THE DADLY

VIRTUES

Adventures from the Worst Job
You'll Ever Love

EDITED BY

JONATHAN
V. LAST

TEMPLETON PRESS

300 Conshohocken State Road, Suite 500
West Conshohocken, PA 19428
www.templetonpress.org

Designed and typeset by Gopa & Ted2 Inc.

Library of Congress Cataloging-in-Publication Data
on file.

Printed in the United States of America

15 16 17 18 19   10 9 8 7 6 5 4 3 2 1

For Cody John Paul, my best buddy

Contents

Acknowledgments

I'VE WANTED TO write a book about fatherhood for a long while—since just after the birth of my son, actually. I was spectacularly unprepared for the moment and needed, desperately, a guide to the job.

The problem is that my kids are still reasonably young—two, five, and seven—so I haven't been able to see very far over the fatherhood horizon. The truth is, I'm not really equipped to write a fatherhood book just yet. But last year I edited a book for the Templeton Press called *The Seven Deadly Virtues*, and it was so much fun that a week or two after it came out the publisher asked if we might do a sequel. Which is when I realized that there was an easy way to do my book about fatherhood. All I had to do was get the band back together and have my favorite writers write it for me. Jackpot.

So if you read *The Seven Deadly Virtues*, most of the faces in this book will be familiar: P. J. O'Rourke, Larry Miller, Jonah Goldberg, James Lileks, Joe Queenan, Iowahawk, and Michael Graham are all back. Toby Young and Joseph Epstein are new additions, because some of the contributors to *The Seven Deadly Virtues* couldn't do this book, on account of their not being fathers. But I've admired Toby and Joe for years and am honored to have them on the squad. Rob Long *was* with us on the other book and isn't a dad—isn't even married. But that actually made him the perfect person to write the chapter on marriage this time around. He's like Jane Goodall among the apes.

I love all my writers equally, but Andrew Ferguson, Christopher Caldwell, Matt Labash, Tucker Carlson, Steve Hayes, and Matt Continetti occupy a special place in my heart. I met all of them through my day job at the *Weekly Standard* before I had kids. Before I was married. They are the ones I've always gone to for advice about the important things in life: writing and parenting. And over the years they've given me guidance, solace, and alcohol, as needed. Getting to write a book with them about fatherhood has been a great gift.

For this gift I have Susan Arellano to thank. She and her team at Templeton Press, especially Trish Vergilio, made this entire project possible. I wouldn't have attempted a book like this without a friend like Susan riding shotgun. And of course, there wouldn't be a Templeton Press without the generous support of the Templeton Foundation and Sir John Templeton. Many thanks to them as well.

There are other debts for *The Dadly Virtues*. I've only met Harvey Mansfield once, but it was enough to leave a deep mark on me. He has influenced my thinking, not just on manliness and fatherhood, but about much else as well.

My dear wife, Shannon, has given me all that is good in my life; without her there would be no sun. She is everything to me. And in addition to all of that, she is, as always, my editor of first and last resort.

My two girls, Cordelia and Emma, loom large in this book, even though they lurk just off the page. I was unready for many aspects of fatherhood, including how deeply I fell in love with them. They are my princesses and my best friends.

My final thanks goes to my oldest, Cody. When the nurse first handed him to me, he stared up from his swaddle with wide eyes. And I told him that everything was different now, and that no matter what, we would always have each other. I love you, my prince. All the way.

—JVL

The Dadly Virtues

Introduction

On Fatherhood, Manliness, and Failure

Jonathan V. Last

DIGNITY IS a delicate fortification.

I was once reasonably dignified. I dressed like a gentleman and luxuriated in the cultural heritage of Western civilization. My three places of residence—my home, my office, and my mind—were free of clutter and arranged in such a way as to allow me to both suck the marrow from my days and nibble at the edges of intellectual life. Then I became a father.

One afternoon I was changing my infant son's diaper when he began micturating. Not in a feeble stream, but in a great, turbo-charged geyser, like one of the fountains in front of the Bellagio. As was his wont. So I reached over, cupped my hand above his manhood, and waited in quiet satisfaction as he peed on me. I was pleased—genuinely, the way I once might have been after finishing, say, *Middlemarch*—that my reflexes had prevented him from spraying the wall and nearby bookshelf. The dismantling of my dignity took three weeks, give or take. I don't keep strict count of these things. Not anymore.

It was around this moment when I began to realize that the primary effect of children is that they take things from you. It begins with sleep, time, and dignity and then expands over the years to include sanity, serenity, and a great deal of money. This is an observation, not a complaint. It's just what they do. In that way, children are like the aging process itself: an exercise in letting go of the ancillary parts of your existence until you are stripped bare, and what remains is your most elemental core. Your soul. Jews celebrate this in the Suffering Servant songs in Isaiah. Christians refer to it as the Way of the Cross. A consultant from McKinsey would call it addition by subtraction.

I'm not going to lie to you. In fatherhood there is much—so much—to be lost. But there is much to be gained, too.

Which is, more or less, what this book is about. *The Dadly Virtues* is something of a Swiss Army knife: part instructional guide, part meditation, part war journal. It is, frankly, the book I wish I'd had back when my first child, Cody, was born. It begins with P. J. O'Rourke talking about turkey basters. It ends with Joseph Epstein ruminating on grandfatherhood. And in between, it encapsulates every major moment along the way, from helping with homework, to first dates, to the awful day when your child moves back home after you've spent a quarter million dollars on college. You'll laugh. You'll cry. You'll want to be a dad all over again.

But before we get to the good stuff, I'd like to spend a moment talking about a subject that often seems diametrically opposed to the indignities of fatherhood: manliness. (You can skip ahead if you like; P. J. is just a few pages away, and there won't be a test.)

There is a school of thought that views the idea of manliness—and even men themselves—as obsolete, or unnecessary, or perhaps even harmful. You can see it in contemporary books, such as Hanna Rosin's *The End of Men* (which is more celebration than lamentation), but it stretches back a ways. At the height of the suffrage movement, for instance, Charlotte Perkins Gilman wrote a novel called *Herland* in which three male explorers stumble upon a lost society comprised entirely of women. It's paradise. Until the men muck everything up. Obviously.

For thousands of years masculinity and femininity were the (literal) yin and yang of the world—the sensibilities that created harmony at every level, from the societal to the personal. As such, the modern push to downgrade one-half of the human condition has created some confusion. On the one hand, it's now socially acceptable for men in their early twenties to wear footy pajamas. Which suggests surrender. On the other hand, there has emerged a self-conscious "men's movement." What began with drumming and sweat lodges has since expanded to include Brooklyn hipsters paying for facial-hair transplants. It often manifests in a talk-radio-friendly form, such as Dr. Helen Smith's book *Men on Strike*, or the collection of websites known as the "manosphere." The men's movement is fighting what it sees as a feminizing culture, with men asserting themselves as manly men. It frequently involves complaining about child custody laws and bad divorce settlements. Not that I'm judging.

Any way you slice it, manliness is in a patch of trouble—we'll talk about that in a moment. Yet despite everything, manliness remains an indispensible, vibrant quality that shapes the world in ways large and small. Consider two men: Dave Karnes and Aleksandr Solzhenitsyn.

You probably know about Solzhenitsyn, a dissident and writer who was one of the five or six most consequential figures of the last century. But perhaps you do not know the details. He was born in Russia in 1918, a bad time in a hard place. In 1945 he was arrested, tortured, and sent to a Gulag for criticizing the Soviet regime in a private letter. During his internment he began what would become his life's work—a series of novels and poems dissecting communism and erecting a moral framework for opposing it. He wrote in secret, while doing hard labor, under the threat of further torture. And, by the way, while battling the early stages of cancer. During one stretch he composed an epic poem, *The Trail*—it's more than seven thousand lines long—entirely in his head because he had neither pen nor paper.

When Solzhenitsyn was released, he continued writing. As his work began to leak out in samizdat form, it exposed the Soviet Gulag to the world. He was eventually labeled a "nonperson." In 1971 the KGB tried to poison him. He survived, so a few years later they exiled him. The communists were right to be afraid of Solzhenitsyn, because he wasn't just trying to pull the veil off of the Iron Curtain. He was fighting for the soul of his people by articulating a vision of what it meant to be Russian. That's manliness.

Dave Karnes showed his steel on a smaller scale. A retired Marine, he was working as an accountant in Connecticut on September 11, 2001. When he heard the news, he left his office and went to a barbershop, where he got his hair buzzed high and tight. Then he went home and put on an old uniform. Then he went to church, where he asked his pastor to pray for him. And then, with his errands complete, he drove forty-one miles south to Manhattan, where he passed himself off as an "official" rescuer and set to work combing the ruins looking for survivors. In this smoldering graveyard Karnes met Chuck Sereika, another man who had come to help out on his own.

Karnes and Sereika spent hours picking their way through the twisted steel and shifting rubble, calling out, over and over, "United States Marines . . . If you can hear us, yell or tap." They were alone, because the official rescue teams had been called off the pile. The conditions were deemed too dangerous. Around 7:00 p.m., Karnes and Sereika heard voices. It took them three hours, but eventually they dug out the last two survivors of the attack, Will Jimeno and John McLoughlin, who had been trapped twenty feet underground.

"Manliness brings change or restores order at moments when routine is not enough, when the plan fails, when the whole idea of rational control by modern science develops leaks," explains the political philosopher Harvey Mansfield. "Manliness is the next-to-last resort, before resignation and prayer." Which is a perfect description of what Solzhenitsyn and Karnes did, each in his own way.

The problem is that manliness has a dark side. "Manliness can also be vainly boastful," Mansfield cautions, "prone to meaningless scuffling and unfriendly." It can drive quarrels and conflicts for small reasons, bad reasons, or no reason at all. Thugs and bullies are manly. I would even go so far as to say that Josef Stalin and Mohammad Atta, who forced Solzhenitsyn and Karnes into action, were acting from manliness. So manliness can be a source of troubles, and a cure for them, too. Mansfield is probably the greatest exponent of manliness since Plato, and even he admits that, on the whole, manliness "seems to be about fifty-fifty good and bad." For every Wyatt Earp, there is a Johnny Ringo; for every Fitzwilliam Darcy, a George Wickham.

The question we should ask ourselves, then, is whether there is anything that unifies the good parts of manliness. And indeed there is. If you drill all the way down to the nuclear core of manliness, Professor Mansfield says, what you find is a familiar impulse: chivalry.

The chivalric nature of manliness reasserts itself through history, from the knight, to the samurai, to the soldier. Why? Because, as Mansfield explains, "Masculinity must prove itself and do so before an audience. It is understood often to be an act of sacrifice against one's interest, hence concerned with honor and shame rather than money and calculation."

If you wanted to distill these two big, interlocking concepts, you'd say that manliness is chivalry. And that chivalry is the impulse to seek honor by protecting the weak and the innocent. What you have just described, then, is the essence of fatherhood. We might even take this a bit further: Fatherhood isn't just manliness. It's the purest form of the *good* side of manliness, the side that brings light into the world.

If you wanted to get *really* metaphysical about the whole thing, you'd note that this link between manliness and fatherhood goes even deeper. The Greeks originated the concept of *thumos*—it literally means "spiritedness." It is *thumos*, Mansfield says, "that induces humans, and especially manly men, to risk their lives in order to save their lives."

So this, finally, is fatherhood: We destroy our lives so that life will continue anew, with part of our selves baked into it. In the ordinary way, of course, through our DNA. But also in the transcendent way, through the ideas and truths and loves that we teach our children.

When I say "fatherhood," I refer to the raising and caring for, as opposed to the siring of, children. And in this regard, men have, to a shameful degree, abdicated their posts. When we talk about the decline of manliness, it's not just the footy pajamas that should worry us. The single worst thing men have done over the last two generations is to abandon their families: Today, 40 percent of children in America are born out of wedlock—that is to say, without a father standing there, committed to help raise them.

That number is worse than you think. In America, only about 69 percent of kids live in a home with two parents. How do we stack up with the rest of the world? In 2014 the World Family Map project looked at the forty-nine countries that make up the vast majority of the world's population. The percentage of children who live with two parents is 88 percent in the Netherlands, 85 percent in the Philippines and Indonesia, 83 percent in Germany, 78 percent in Canada, 76 percent in Nigeria—*Nigeria*—74 percent in Ethiopia, and 72 percent in Bolivia. With our 69 percent, the United States sits in thirty-second place. We beat out Uganda. Barely.

If you believe that (1) manliness can be problematic, yet is essential for a society; and (2) the positive aspects of manliness stem in large part from fatherhood, then this abandonment is, as the philosophers might note, a Very Bad Thing. It would lead to a society that is increasingly callow, nasty, and unpleasant—predisposed to juvenilia, ephemera, and self-centeredness. Does this ring any bells?

All of which is to say that if we are failing as a nation, it may well be because we're failing at manliness. And if we are failing at manliness, it's probably because we're failing at fatherhood.

Now that's a whole lot of grim failure, and I promised you this was going to be a fun, rollicking, good-time of a book. And besides which, I don't mean that you, personally, are responsible for the decline of America. You're a dad! You've done your bit.

You can sit back and smile at the memories as Matthew Continetti recounts the glorious, prelapsarian weeks of pregnancy, and those sweet, sleepy, first days of parenthood. Before the colic set in and the diapers started exploding. Before you were dispatched to ransack CVS at 3:00 a.m. for breast pads and butt paste. Before you felt the urge to punch strangers who sidle up to you at the grocery store while the baby is screaming and tell you to cherish these days "because they go by so fast."

You can applaud Tucker Carlson's inspired parenting as he builds his son a potato cannon—and then shoots his daughters' Barbies out of it. You can sympathize with Toby Young as he massacres his kids' fish mere hours after bringing them home from the pet store. And depending on where you are on the ride, you might even take some pointers from Matt Labash when it's time to tell your kids about the birds and the bees. (Warning: The surgeon general has determined that taking sex-talk advice from Matt Labash can be hazardous to your marriage.)

And if you've made it through the grind of changing diapers and packing lunches and driving to practice and scaring off potential boyfriends, you can sit in the afterglow and revise history with Joseph Epstein. Remember, there's always grandfatherhood to look forward to. If you make it.

Like I said, this is the book I wish I'd had when Cody was born because it covers just about every lesson you'll need to survive fatherhood, except one: failure.

I fear I have been—or will be—a terrible, colossal failure as a father. In part, this is because I've been obsessed with the *idea* of failure for a very long time. It began in kindergarten with a thin, prissy, middle-aged teacher named Mr. Bloomfield. Reared to worship at the altar of academic achievement, I worked hard at kindergarten, convinced that once you hit five, everything from there on out would go on your permanent record. When my first report card was sent home, Mr. Bloomfield awarded me "outstanding" on all counts: "sits still," "listens," "washes his hands after using the bathroom." With one exception. When it came to "cutting in straight lines," he marked me as "needs improvement." Thus Mr. Bloomfield and I began our cold war.

I was furious. I was an ace with scissors, and having been programmed from an early age to be a doctor, I became convinced that Mr. Bloomfield was trying to keep me out of medical school. After that first report card I would march up to Mr. Bloomfield every time we used the shears, show him my work, and demand that he acknowledge the cuts were straight. His displeasure was evident even to my five-year-old self. I went to a different school the next year.

This preoccupation with failure followed me through my youth, through high school, and finally to college. It haunted me through physics (which was difficult), and organic chemistry (which was horrible), and physical chemistry (which was the worst of both worlds). It chased me as I studied for the MCATs. And then it devoured me whole as I was rejected from medical schools from sea to shining sea.

At which point I ended up writing for a living. (It turns out that there is no test to see who's allowed to scribble down words. They'll let *anyone* into this racket.) And then I left the idea of failure behind for a good long while. In fact, I didn't really think about it again until I was staring down the barrel of a baby. Everyone always says that being a parent is the hardest job in the world. I figured that it would be hard in the way that organic chemistry was hard: that it was a task that could be mastered through a combination of intelligence and diligence. I had beaten organic chemistry, so I could crush parenthood. You can imagine my surprise.

A few months after Cody was born, I sat visiting with my wife and my friend Chris, who has been my best mate since childhood. It was late in the evening, and I was trying to convey to him what I had learned thus far about being a father.

"You see," I explained, "it turns out that it's not *hard work* in the intellectual sense. It's not rocket science where some people can figure it out and others can't. No, it's *hard work* in the way that digging a ditch is hard. Anyone can dig a ditch. There's no way to dig smarter. Or dig faster. Having a baby is like being assigned to dig a ditch. That goes all the way to the horizon."

"Okay," Chris replied warily. "But it's good, right? You're glad you did it?"

"Sure," I said. "It's like going to the dentist. Everyone dreads the dentist. And it's no fun. But when you're seventy and still have your teeth, you'll be grateful you went."

I turned to my wife for confirmation. Her face was frozen in horror. "You just compared parenthood to ditch digging and dentistry," she said evenly.

It was at this point I realized I might be doing fatherhood wrong.

From this first moment of failure have sprung many others—I do keep a strict count of *these* things. And I think a lot about how to raise Cody so that he doesn't wind up like me.

Teaching children about failure is one of our more subtle responsibilities. Nearly everyone encounters failure in life, but people respond differently to it. Some learn; some are strengthened; some are broken. It depends on the person. It also depends on when the failure hits. Too soon and you might become habituated to it. Too late and you might not have time to recover. There's probably a sweet spot in life where people are well equipped to absorb large-scale failure but also have ample time to emerge from it. Unfortunately, we have little control over when failure will visit our children. But we can try to prepare them nonetheless.

There are different schools of thought on the matter. One holds that failures ought to be imposed early and often, almost like hazing. Think of this as the Basic Training view, where you break them down so that you can build them up. The opposite school is best articulated by the businessman and sometime philosopher Peter Thiel. "One of the ideas I'm very skeptical of is that people learn from failure," he says. "I think, in practice, failure's really demotivating. Hopefully, you have the character to persevere and keep going, but I think the default is that failure is powerfully demotivating."

Aside from the motivational aspect, Thiel thinks failure is overrated because its causes are often too complicated to yield any real lessons. When a kid gets a bad grade in organic chemistry—just to pick an example at random—is it because he didn't work hard enough? Or because he's not good at the subject? Or because the teacher did a lousy job? Or because he was stretched too thin with other work? What should he learn from his failure: Study more? Take easier classes? Find another major?

To my mind, when it comes to failure, what we really want to teach our children is how not to internalize it. Of course, the only way to learn this skill is to fail a number of times. There's the rub. Fortunately, there's an institution devoted to helping fathers and their children master this duality. It's called baseball.

As George Will, Donald Kagan, and other philosophers have noted, baseball is the high church of ritualized failure. A great team will lose one out of every three games. A player who fails at the plate 70 percent of the time will go to the Hall of Fame. One of the game's key statistics is actually called "errors." And baseball's failure is the best sort because its instances are routinized and discrete, which means that you can actually learn from them. *Why didn't I hit that pitch?* Because you were too early. *Why did the grounder get past me?* Because you didn't touch your glove all the way to the dirt. No big deal; happens all the time. Let's try again.

If you want to teach your children to manage failure, you should make baseball part of your life with them. It doesn't really matter how you do it, whether it's playing Little League, watching the pros, or just having catch in the yard.

We have a minor league team a couple miles down the road from our house, so I started taking Cody to games when he was two—young enough to still be in diapers but old enough to enjoy peanuts and Cracker Jack. The next spring I started giving him batting practice in the front yard with one of the red, plastic fat bats that generations of kids have grown up with. When he turned five, I got him a glove. I don't know if this will be enough to shield him from a life filled with the fear of failure. But it's something. It's a start.

Sometimes when I see Cody struggle and get frustrated with schoolwork, my heart breaks a little. We want our children to have only the best parts of ourselves inside them; it seems cruel that they should have to inherit our faults. But it's a long game, and there are a lot of innings in life. What we have to remember is that winning the pennant in fatherhood doesn't mean that we do everything perfectly. It means getting enough things right that your kid still loves you after he's grown up. That he still looks forward to having a catch.

One more story about baseball: When I first started taking Cody to games, our routine was always the same: We'd get to the ballpark in the middle of the second, stay for a few innings, as long as his interest held, and then head home. The first time we made it to the end of a game, Cody was four. He looked at me quizzically and said, "Wait—baseball is *over*?" I realized that, from his perspective, baseball had always been happening. We got to the stadium and they were playing baseball; we left to go home and they were playing baseball. It wasn't something that had a beginning and end. To him, baseball was like the ocean—omnipresent, the tides always rolling in.

Which leads me to an observation about fatherhood. A man with no children can easily be lulled into the sense that time is standing still. It is not. It is marching past you, relentlessly. Having a child growing and changing before your eyes makes this unavoidably clear. It's depressing. But also necessary. Because it means that your time on earth won't sneak past you. And if you're living well, it helps you focus on not wasting the time you have.

As I said at the beginning, fatherhood costs us a great deal.

Every hour you spend driving your minivan to Babies"R"Us is an hour you can't be sleeping, or watching football, or reading Dostoevsky. And in truth, I'm not sure the ditch-digging metaphor is entirely wrong. Much of childrearing—the tantrums, and the sibling rivalry, and trying to get them to sleep, and *will you please eat your dinner already!*—is deeply unpleasant. But to paraphrase James Madison, if children were angels, fatherhood would be unnecessary.

If you take anything from this book, I hope it's that the struggle is worth it. As a general rule I try not to talk in the conditional mood, especially when it comes to family life. Everyone has their own circumstances, and I respect that. I really do. But if you aren't otherwise engaged in some duty that precludes it—say, the priesthood—and you have the opportunity, then you should be a father. There is nothing more vexing, exhausting, noble, or manly.

It's the worst job you'll ever love.

CHAPTER 1

What Do Men Get from Fatherhood?

Besides What They Put In . . .

P. J. O'Rourke

BABIES ARE OUTPUT. Input must be considered.

The single strongest motivation, object, aim, intent, and goal of men between the ages of Nintendo Wii obsession and wheeled walkers is to do a thing that makes babies (or a thing that, in the abstract, is similar to it).

Thus we already know what men *got* out of fatherhood even if, "conceptionally speaking," a turkey baster was involved.

But that is fatherhood in the technical sense. Not that technical sense isn't necessary to fatherhood. Correctly installing the Graco SnugRide infant seat in the back of your minivan requires an advanced degree in mechanical engineering from MIT.

There are, however, general as well as specialized aspects to fatherhood. Generally, "fatherhood" requires a father. A father who is present and accounted for and actively engaged in raising his kids. Or her kids, because nowadays a father may be of the mother gender, just as a mother may be of the father gender, and the kids, for all I know, are transgender. Believe me, it doesn't make any difference. When it's 3:00 a.m. and you're trying to burp a colicky baby while *It's Sew Easy* is on PBS and Rebecca Kemp Brent is putting the final touches on a tucked bolster pillow and you can't find the remote to change channels, sex will be the last thing on your mind.

(Some advice: Try holding the baby upside-down and kissy-kissy-wissy on itsum-bitsome's tummy-ummy. That might earn you a belch, and hence some peace and quiet. Or the kid might—mercifully—throw up on the Bugs Bunny bedroom slippers you got for Father's Day. Or you might find the TV remote, which baby has been teething on, and shake it loose.)

One thing men do not get from fatherhood is much sleep. When the worry about the baby crying ceases, the worry about the baby not breathing begins. Then, as baby grows, there are midnight coughs and midnight colds, midnight bed wets, midnight climbings into bed with you (followed by midnight bed wets), midnight demands for a drink of water, midnight fears of things in the closet, midnight snacks, midnight sneaks to the Nintendo, and, before you know it, baby is sixteen and has a driver's license and it's midnight and baby isn't home yet.

So what's in this for me?

Your manhood—or your social construct of male identity, or whatever—has been affirmed. You got someone knocked up. You are a big, swinging turkey baster.

And right here is where many fathers stop. Tempting. And it's probably tempting to mothers to let fathers stop right here, too. Mothers have myriad roles to play in life—nurturer, comforter, healer, educator, inspiration, example, sole support, saint, next president of the United States. Men bump and run.

Men have only one role. They provide a sperm cell who goes where men want to go but takes it to the next level. After that, men are dispensable and can drink, smoke, talk sports, commit crimes, and fight wars.

Fatherhood gives men something to do. If it were not for fathers, real fathers, the world outside the home would be one big cigar bar full of drunk vets with PTSD planning bank heists.

And there would be—although women would deny that this is possible—even more sports-talk radio.

Fatherhood introduces men to worry. Worry is not something that comes naturally to men or something we can learn to do on our own. Men know about fear. We can be afraid to jump off the roof of a speeding SUV onto a pile of discarded mattresses. But we have a cure for that. "Hold my beer. Now watch this!"

It would never occur to us to *worry* about the speeding SUV or the pile of discarded mattresses. We don't get *worried* until we become fathers. Our woman begins to grow huge. She acquires strange appetites. We worry. Is she going to eat us?

Then we worry that we have to go into the hospital, even though we're feeling fine—indeed quite fine, after three slugs from the vodka bottle when contractions began.

And, more worrisome yet, they want us to go into the delivery room despite the fact that *we're* not pregnant and no matter how much we explain that we're a lot better at pacing up and down hospital waiting rooms, smoking Lucky Strikes, and paging through decades-old copies of *Field & Stream* than we are at helping to deliver babies. Which—and this is a real worry—they also want us to do. (More advice: *Stay up by your woman's head! Stay up by her head! For God's sake, stay up by her head!*)

We worry that the mom is going to die. We worry that the baby is going to die. We worry that, if we don't get more vodka, we're going to die. Welcome to the next twenty-eight years of living, including grad school and the couple of years when the kid moves back in with you "while I find myself."

I say you're in Williamsburg, Brooklyn, with the rest of the kids your age, and I say go to Williamsburg and look for yourself there.

Fatherhood introduces men to responsibility, which has also previously been a stranger. No matter how many responsibilities men are supposed to have, we will never, left to our own devices, meet them personally until we are fathers. And, now that we're fathers, the "own devices" that we are "left to" are Graco SnugRide infant seats.

> Mr. Traffic Patrol Policeman: "Sir, are you responsible for the installation of this infant seat in the back of your minivan?"
> You: "Officer, I swear those are brand-new bungee cords."

Fatherhood explains love to men. Previously men used *love* as a technical term meaning "roll in the hay." Then comes Snookums. And there's not even a proper word for the love you feel. The classical Greeks divided love into four kinds: *Eros* is certainly not what we're talking about. Nor is *philia*, brotherly love. Nor *agape*, benevolent love of the whole world (from the Greek *gape*, meaning, "had too much wine"). Nor *storge*, which means mere affection or acceptance or putting up with someone. That's the kind of love the baby's mother feels for you.

Herodotus, a classical Greek, says in *The Histories* that among the Persians, "Before the age of five a boy lives with the women and never sees his father, the object being to spare the father distress if the child should die in the early stages of its upbringing. In my view this is a sound practice." (Which proves that American public schools might be better than we think and that perhaps *too much* Herodotus is being taught to students from trailer parks and the inner city.)

Fatherhood presents things for men to fulminate about, fulmination being a favorite activity of the mature male. Those public school educations, for instance. It's bad enough that they're teaching kids to read that old liar Herodotus. But when they start teaching kids that FDR was a role model for differently-abled persons who excel in life. . .

"Excel in life, my behind," I fulminate when the kids get home from school. "That communistic, skirt-chasing gimp kept the fact that he was in a wheelchair secret from the public for forty-four years! And don't even get me started on the New Deal! His darn cousin Teddy's Square Deal had already ruined the nation! Then Teddy Roosevelt ran on the Bull Moose third-party ticket in 1912, depriving America of one of its finest and most decent chief executives—and role model for all of us differently waistlined persons—William Howard Taft, thereby allowing the wet-smack, buttinski, warmongering, racist Woodrow Wilson to. . . ." But it seems the kids have wandered from the room.

On the other hand, your children's education sends you back to school again. And this time I was determined to learn something. I followed my children's schoolwork carefully and did fine through the sixth-grade vocabulary quizzes and the multiplication table, up to 7 x 7. Fortunately my kids have been taking Spanish, and I already know all the Spanish I need to know:

"Uno más cerveza fría, por favor."

And:

"¿Donde es el baño por los hombres?"

But then we got to middle school math and there was Chief Soh-Cah-Toa lurking in the primeval forest of Trig, right where he'd scalped me almost fifty years before. Now when my children are studying after school I just tell them, "Beats me. Google it."

Fatherhood provides men with a home. I was a bachelor until my late forties. I had a *house*—a little house in the woods. There were shotguns and fishing rods propped in the corners. My fly-tying vice was screwed into the dining room tabletop. Firewood was stacked in the kitchen cabinets, conveniently near the woodstove. The chainsaw was in the bathtub. (It leaked oil if I left it on the floor.) And the refrigerator was stocked with beer, bait, cans of hash, a skillet, ammo, and more beer. (Not that cans of hash, skillets, and ammo need to be refrigerated.

But putting them in the refrigerator meant I always knew where to find them.) Décor was taxidermy animals and unframed Helmut Newton photographs.

Now I have a home. The refrigerator is filled with yogurt, fruit juice, skim milk, vitamin water, turkey bacon, and what I initially took for a houseplant, but turns out to be "kale." The kitchen cabinets are stacked with five-grain breads, seven-grain breads, nine-grain breads, and breads of grains to the nth power—none of them containing trans fats. Central heating and air-conditioning has been installed, lest the children somehow be baked in the woodstove the way Hansel and Gretel almost were by the Wicked Witch. Wicked Witches being poor role models for parenting. The shotguns are in a closet with a Yale lock on the door. Willow Ware covers the dining room table. Rubber ducks are in the bathtub. And the Helmut Newton photographs have been replaced with pictures of babes of an entirely different type.

Fatherhood defines bravery for men. We thought it involved beer. Now it has a larger meaning. And still involves beer. I have two teenage girls. I'm having a brass plaque engraved for my front door:

> This is my house. I am O'Rourke.
> Well-armed, well-oiled, and choleric.
> These are my daughters. Lay not a hand
> Upon them. Now, get off my land.

My children are adored. And they give as good as they get. No one else "adores" a man. A woman (who has lost her contacts *and* had too many Jell-O shots) may think we're "hot." A man, if he gets a look at the way we secured the infant seat with bungee cords, may think we're "cool." A mom may think we're "good"—when she's talking to another mother who has a son in jail. But Baby thinks the sun shines through our burp cloth. Who else can throw Baby so high in the air and (usually) catch him or her? Who else can get down on the playroom floor and (too plausibly) imitate the Hungry Hungry Hippo? You can prolong this adoration of the almost supernatural powers of the father, if you try. For example, learn to burp the alphabet. The kids will adore you all their lives. (If they're boys. My seventeen-year-old daughter has told me in no uncertain terms not to burp the alphabet in front of her friends.)

Fatherhood makes men proud. Proud of everything your kids do and say. Recently I was deploring the exceedingly messy state of my children's bedrooms and gently urging them to "PUT EVERYTHING BACK WHERE IT CAME FROM!!!"

"What if it came from the floor?" was my ten-year-old son's rejoinder. He'll be chief justice of the Supreme Court someday.

A father always has someone to play with. I play "Hide-the-Car-Keys" with my seventeen-year-old daughter. I play *Carrie* (the original 1976 version) on the DVD over and over again for my fourteen-year-old daughter, so she'll know how to handle bullying at school. And nobody but my ten-year-old son will spend hours in the backyard tossing a baseball instead of doing his homework, or me doing his homework, or me doing my work, or him writing this. Actually our Labrador retriever will play catch, too. But it's hard to get the mitt on her nose and she throws like a girl.

Speaking of which, a father gets to pass along his sports skills and knowledge to his children. "When you're batting," I tell my son, "always pull your lead foot away from home plate. Put 'your foot in the bucket,' as they call it. That way you won't get hit by the pitch." And I tell him, "When you're playing outfield and the other team has a man on third and a man on first and the batter hits a grounder to you, throw the ball to the pitcher. He'll know what to do with it." Things like that.

A father always has someone to laugh at his jokes. For example, when you're driving by a cemetery you say, "The graveyard is the most popular spot in town."

"Why?" the kids will say.

"*People are dying to get in.*"

And the kids will laugh. (If they're boys. My daughters reminded me that we were on our way to Great Aunt Dotty's funeral.)

Plus you can make everybody else laugh with the hilarious things that your kids are always saying. I remember one time when my eldest daughter had just started to talk, and my wife took her to the grocery store. When they came out of the store it was pouring. My wife was standing in the rain outside the minivan, trying to get my daughter buckled into that infant seat I told you about. And my daughter was wiggling around and not cooperating at all, and my wife said, "Mommy is starting to get mad."

To which my daughter replied, "*And wet, too.*"

That one's immortal. And so are you. Fatherhood means your chromosomes will eternally replicate and you will, in a sense, live on and, in a way, perhaps achieve everything you ever hoped for. Such as being president of the United States. I mean, "*And wet, too*"? That girl will be Hillary Clinton someday.

You live forever. Or maybe it just seems like forever. I'm sixty-seven with three children under eighteen. I just did some math. I'm going to get a huge drink. But I'm also going to get—assuming grad school and a couple of years of finding himself for the youngest—huge bills to pay until 2043.

CHAPTER 2

Newborn Terror

The Moment You Realize That "Bundle of Joy" Is
a Euphemism for Something Very Different

Matthew Continetti

EVER SINCE my son was born ten months ago, I've been thinking of a scene from *Star Trek IV: The Voyage Home.*

The valiant crew of the starship *Enterprise* has commandeered
a Klingon bird-of-prey for their return to planet Earth. Spock,
the Vulcan science officer who has just come back from the
dead—it's a long story—is on the bridge, where he is monitoring interstellar communications. His longtime friend Leon-
ard "Bones" McCoy, the ship's doctor, approaches him and sits
down.

"Perhaps we could cover some philosophical ground,"
McCoy says, hoping to start a conversation about mortality.
"Life, death, life. Things of that nature."

"I did not have time on Vulcan to review the philosophical
disciplines," Spock says.

"C'mon, Spock. It's me, McCoy. You really have gone where
no man has gone before. Can't you tell me what it felt like?"

"It would be impossible," Spock says, "to discuss the subject
without a common frame of reference."

McCoy is flabbergasted.

"You're joking," he says.

"A joke—is a story with a humorous climax?"

"You mean I have to *die* to discuss your insights on death?"

My attitude toward fatherhood is the same as Spock's attitude toward resurrection. It is impossible to understand unless it is happening—or has already happened—to you. Becoming a father changes one's life so quickly, so substantively, and so comprehensively, one finds it increasingly difficult to identify with, or relate to, single friends and couples who have not crossed the barrier separating the carefree, childfree life from the duty-bound, child-saturated one.

For example: The other day I asked a single friend of mine what his plans were for the evening. He and his girlfriend maintain a busy social schedule, and I wanted to know if he was free for an impromptu business meeting.

"Well," he told me, "we're thinking of meeting for a drink."

"Ah," I said. "With whom?"

My friend, not having reached the point in life where leaving the house requires an amount of logistical preparation similar to that which preceded the invasion of Normandy, looked upon me with pity.

"With each other," he said.

With each other—what a concept! What would have been a commonplace activity for me less than a year ago is now an alien ritual, as distant from the day-to-day realities of my life as a rain dance by an Amazonian tribe. Reflecting on my new reality—the cycle of work and drinks replaced by the cycle of work, baby, more baby, and drinks at home to forget about baby—I find solace in the thought that my friend's time will also come, that at some point, he too will suffer that loss of freedom, that death of personality, known as "fatherhood."

The tragedy is that he cannot begin to comprehend his fate. There is no way for him to prepare, to study, to fortify himself for what is coming. Taking in a movie, reading for pleasure, bingeing on Netflix, spending days with no set appointments, no fixed routines—all these distractions are nice while they last. Once the baby arrives, you can say arrivederci, sayonara, au revoir, good-bye to living for one's self, auf Wiedersehen to looking out for numero uno.

Maybe one day the crew of the *Enterprise* will bring us dads, like Spock, back from the grave. But for the next twenty years or so—a sentence that is extended with the birth of each additional child—you are no longer the star of your own movie. You are a supporting player, the straight man to baby's comic antics, Felix to his Oscar. Better start learning your lines.

This disassociation of self begins prior to the birth of your child. For most of my wife's pregnancy I practiced denial, living as if our existence as married yuppies would continue uninterrupted, and enjoying the perks of having, for nine months, a go-to designated driver. It was not until several weeks before my son came into this world that I had the first hint of what life with him would be like.

My wife had signed us up for a labor and delivery class at the hospital where our baby would be born. The class was held on a Saturday. As we drove to the hospital that clear and sunny winter morning—my memory here is fuzzy, and those who know me best will tell you I am not one to complain—I *may* have griped about spending 50 percent of the weekend inside a classroom.

Then again, I said, maybe 50 percent is something of an exaggeration. "How long is this class, anyway?"

"Not long," my wife answered. "Eight hours."

We arrived at the hospital and followed signs to the classroom. We would be spending the day in a large, windowless meeting space with a dry-erase board and video screen. Some two dozen folding chairs were arranged in a circle. On one side of the room was a table that held juice and snacks. We filled out name tags as other expecting couples took their seats. Husbands and wives murmured to each other. A recording of Enya was playing. I checked my watch.

The instructor was a nurse and grandmother. She began the class by asking the dads to step out of the room while she spoke to the moms, probably to turn them against us.

"Take this pen and paper," she said to one of the men. "And write down all of the questions you have."

The dads shuffled out to the hallway and formed a standing circle. We looked at each other awkwardly. One of us ducked into the men's room—morning sickness, perhaps. I checked my watch.

"So," said the newly appointed secretary, "what are our questions?"

One guy was curious—no doubt for purely medical reasons—about the varieties of painkillers available to his wife. Another guy wanted to know the best time to take his wife to the delivery room. Many of our questions were detail-oriented: What should we have ready at home for the trip to the hospital and for our eventual return? What would be the monetary cost of delivery and our stay at the hospital? Who would handle the birth certificate and Social Security information? Where would we get food? How could we make our wives more comfortable? I wanted to know where to park.

There was one question, however, that I cannot forget; that stood for all of our ignorance and naiveté, a symbol of our fundamental irrelevance to the biological miracle at hand. When his turn came, one of the dads pursed his lips, looked at the floor, raised his head, and said, "What do we do, you know, *after*?"

Silence.

His question was unanswerable. Not having experienced father-hood, we lacked the common frame of reference necessary to express, in even the simplest terms, the shape our lives would take after our families increased by 50 percent. The very idea of a discontinuity between past practices and future responsibilities was, to me at least, a novelty.

I stood there shifting my weight from heel to heel, contemplating the terrifying prospect of assuming responsibility for the life and rearing of a human being, knowing that I myself am not exactly what one would call "fully reared." Eventually the instructor summoned the men to return to the classroom.

Our spouses greeted us with knowing smiles. It quickly became obvious that the objective of class was less to familiarize us with the hospital than to educate the dads in their forthcoming role in the drama of delivery. That role could have been summarized, much more clearly and briefly, as follows: Be nice to your wife. Do what she asks.

The group discussed our questions. The issue of "what comes after" was met with nervous laughter (and remained unanswered). We toured the hospital. We watched clip after clip after clip of "birth stories" in which moms, writhing in agony, assumed semicomical positions while dads gave their wives massages and tried to say nice things and otherwise looked on helplessly. At the end of each story a child was born.

We practiced the exercises ourselves. The one I remember best: The couple pretends it has regressed in age and is at a middle-school dance. You stand there, hands on her hips, her hands on your shoulders, and sway in place as your wife breathes deeply to distract herself from the pain of contractions. As we rehearsed, the instructor walked throughout the room, telling us, in a low, smooth, NPR-like voice, about mindfulness and meditation and support. I checked my watch.

We watched more birth stories. The class sat in the dark, observing one couple after another endure the trial of delivering a baby. Howling, panting, crying, pleading—we heard it all, we saw it all. When the lights came up, no one was smiling. Each pair of husbands and wives seemed to have moved a few inches closer together. Steeling themselves for what lay ahead.

My wife raised her hand.

"Yes?" said the instructor.

"The women in the videos—did they have epidurals?"

"Oh no," said the instructor. "These are *natural* births."

The women in our class let out a very audible collective sigh.

The instructor looked confused. "How many moms here are planning on having an epidural?"

All but one of the women raised their hands.

Poof, voilà—just like that, the class was exposed as a tremendous waste of time. A waste of time that still had three or so hours to run.

Knowing that my wife was going to be heavily anaesthetized during delivery, I let my mind wander. And yet, despite my best efforts to shield it from infiltration, pieces of conversation, snippets of the lecture, random audio—where to park, the importance of breast-feeding, what to bring to the hospital, cafeteria menu options—penetrated my consciousness.

The instructor gave us tips on how to calm an agitated baby. Try changing his diaper, she said. Bounce him gently in your arms. And she kept repeating the phrase "skin-to-skin," to the point where it assumed the status of a mantra, an incantation that became impossible for me to ignore.

"After the baby is delivered, we give him to the mother to hold, because skin-to-skin contact is soothing and calming to the child." "Be sure that you spend a few moments during each feeding enjoying skin-to-skin contact with your baby." "If the child is colicky or fussy, try skin-to-skin." "Skin-to-skin always helps." "We find that babies who enjoy a lot of skin-to-skin time do very well on their SATs." (It's possible I hallucinated that last part.)

I felt as if I had stumbled upon a panacea for every ailment, worry, and nuisance. "Do you suffer from the heartbreak of psoriasis? Then try skin-to-skin!" It was while I was caught up in this reverie that I first began to recognize the scope of change endured by the father of a newborn. There would come a time, it occurred to me, when my wife will have recovered from the delivery and find herself busy with an errand or a get-together with friends to which she could not bring, or would not want to bring, our son.

Which meant that there would come a time, there inevitably would be a *moment*—a suspenseful, awe-inspiring, climactic *moment*—when I, who had never changed a diaper or made a bottle or held a baby for more than a few minutes—would have to take care of our infant myself.

And so I did what any young man would do.

I panicked.

"When's our due date again?" I whispered to my wife.

"March 15," she said.

"March 15. Got it."

"Why are you sweating all of a sudden?"

I checked my watch.

As it turned out, our son was born a few days before the Ides of March. The accommodations at the hospital were comfortable, the nurses were kind, and during night feedings they brought the wrong baby to our room only once. After a few days the three of us returned home.

The best thing about newborns is that they are not very exciting. They tend to sleep a lot. They eat. When they are hungry
they cry. "The truth," writes Dave Barry in *Babies and Other Haz-
ards of Sex*, "is that during the first six months babies mainly just
lie around and poop."

This condition is perfect for dads. To my surprise I discovered that changing diapers is easy as long as the child is a few
weeks old and pretty much inert. As for lying around, well,
that's how I spend most of my free time anyway. I recall one
pleasant and edifying evening my family spent watching *A Few
Good Men*, as I explained to my son, not for the last time, how
Colonel Jessup is actually the hero of the story.

I was also lucky not to lose too much sleep. Our baby is not
colicky. When he awoke at night it was because he was hungry. And since he was being breast-fed, I couldn't do much to
address his needs other than wake up my wife. When I knew
she had things under control, I would fall asleep again. Fatherhood: piece of cake.

One night, when the baby started crying, I awoke and noticed
that it was 4:00 a.m. "Wow," I said to my wife, who was groggily
rising from bed. "This is the first time he's gotten up all night.
Sleep training works!"

She laughed bitterly.

"It's the third time. You slept through the other two."

Sometime in the early months, during one night's second or
third feeding, my wife became understandably frustrated with
this state of affairs. She reiterated the core teaching of the labor
and delivery class, indeed the cardinal rule of the Continetti
home: Be nice to the wife. Do what she asks. So I left the bed,
accompanied her to the nursery, and, half asleep, lay on the
floor until the feeding was over.

As we made our way back to our room, I said that perhaps
next time I could remain asleep, as it was biologically impossible for me to feed the baby until we weaned him off of breast

milk. Nature had decreed, I pronounced, that at this point in his life there was literally nothing I could do to make baby go back to sleep. It therefore made sense for me to rest so I wasn't completely addled during the workday.

My wife narrowed her eyes, shook her head, grimaced, and said, "Why do you have to be so . . . *rational?*"

It was more than rationality that drove me to such conclusions, however. It was fear. I simply did not want to handle the bundle of joy—one of the many baby euphemisms that I now understand to be ironic—on my own. The terrible *moment* of complete responsibility had not yet arrived. I was hoping to delay it for as long as I could.

But I could not delay it forever. The months passed, and one weekend my wife made plans to spend a Saturday afternoon with some girlfriends. I would stay at home. With the child.

"You'll be okay," she said.

I couldn't tell whether that was a question or a statement.

"Sure," I said.

"You'll put him down for a nap," she said. "He'll sleep for most of the time."

"Sure," I said.

"And I'll only be gone for a couple of hours," she said.

"Please don't leave me here," I said.

The afternoon began innocently enough. I read him some books. I gave him a bottle. I placed him in his crib for naptime, turned on the white noise machine, dimmed the lights, and tiptoed out of his room. As I closed the door I listened for any sign of discomfort. All was quiet.

I went downstairs and turned on the television. *Enter the Dragon* was playing on cable. I sat on the couch and stretched my legs. *Not so hard after all*, I thought. Life should be so easy.

Then the wailing began.

Not fussing, not crying, not weeping, but wailing—an excruciating repetitive klaxon that began softly and slowly but built up into a roar of displeasure, an air-raid-siren-like peal of intensity. I ran up the stairs to the nursery, threw the door open, and lifted my son from his crib.

The diaper, I thought: *It must be the diaper.*

I changed the diaper, but the wailing continued. *The pajamas*, I thought: *He must be uncomfortable in the pajamas.* I replaced his pajamas with a fresh pair. Throughout the process he screamed and struggled. The wail did not end.

I tried desperately to recall the offhand remark from the labor and delivery class: Bounce the baby gently in your arms. Move around with him. Remind him of the womb.

We started bouncing. He calmed down slightly. I tried sitting on the exercise ball in the center of the nursery. But he wouldn't have it. He wanted the standing bounce. The standing bounce was what he got.

Still he cried. I tried singing. Usually if I sang loud enough he would quiet down, if for no other reason than shock or disgust.

"Row, row, row your boat, gently down the stream. . . ."

"WAAAAAAAAHHHHHHHH!"

I tried the walking bounce: basically lunge squats with the baby in my arms. We went like this from the nursery to the master bedroom to the office to the guest room. He kept wailing.

Changing, bouncing, and lunging—all useless. The wail continued. I was ready to call my wife, to beg for her assistance. Then another memory from the birth and delivery class hit me.

"Skin-to-skin always helps."

Of course! Holding the hysterical child, I lunge-squatted back to the nursery. I placed him on the changing table and removed his pajama top. Then I took off the T-shirt I was wearing.

"Here we go!" I said. "Skin-to-skin!" I pressed him against me.

"WAAAAAAAAHHHHHHHH!"

Perhaps a combination of skin-to-skin bouncing and lunging would work? I tried it.

Nothing. I was running out of options. I took him downstairs to the kitchen and, bouncing him in one arm, made a fresh bottle. Then shirtless baby, bottle, and shirtless I went to the family room. I would try feeding him again. We sat on the couch.

Which is where my wife found us, two half-naked sleeping messes, Bruce Lee on in the background, when she returned to the house an hour and a half later.

She burst into laughter.

"Skin-to-skin," I said.

I turned my head back to the couch, made sure the snoozing boy was comfortable on my chest, and closed my eyes, suffused with a feeling of pride and happiness, of joy and satisfaction.

It's hard to put that feeling into words. But if you are a dad, you know what I'm talking about.

CHAPTER 3

Siblings
The Best Gift You'll Ever Give Your Kids

Stephen F. Hayes

I HAD ONLY a second to decide.

Ten years earlier I would have been able to execute the kind of vaulting leap I was contemplating—from a seated position, across a cafeteria table—without much of a problem. But it was a few months before my fortieth birthday and I wasn't in great shape. My weight fluctuates by the season. Every spring and summer, I ride hundreds of miles on my bike so that by the time fall sets in, I've slimmed down from "obese" to merely "overweight" on the federal government's body mass index chart.

But it was February. So I was fat. The waistlines on my pants were tight. The well-worn belt-hole from the trim months sat empty while the buckle on my belt bulged as the prong strained in the last very last hole, fighting desperately to contain me. During the winter months, I have to rock back and forth a few times whenever I want to get out of my Volkswagen Jetta—in order to generate some momentum.

All of which was part of the equation as I calculated whether to try jumping across the table to stop my son before he could embarrass me. Had it been August, I might have tried. But it wasn't. So with a sense of resignation I sat, helpless, as he began to speak.

The woman he was addressing was probably seventy years old. And probably 250 pounds. Maybe she had the same seasonal weight shifts I did. I wasn't judging her. She was a nurse, and we were at a hospital, in the cafeteria where I was grabbing lunch with my three-year-old son, Conner, and my five-year-old daughter, Grace, while my wife rested in her room, having just given birth to a beautiful little creature we named Jane. The nurse—a gentle soul with a warm, welcoming presence—had just asked Grace and Conner why they were wearing capes. And Conner explained, with his sister adding details, that their mom had gotten them Super Brother and Super Sister capes in anticipation of the arrival of their new sibling.

Conner was a child born without a filter. He said whatever occurred to him at precisely the moment it occurred to him. This led to some uncomfortable moments. He told the cashier at our local bagel shop that her lip piercing looked "stupid." (He was right.) He asked a woman at the doctor's office if her eye patch meant she was a pirate. (It did not.) He wondered aloud if a dwarf he saw at the grocery store was short because he didn't like his vegetables. (Sigh.)

At the hospital, Conner went on and on about the capes and how he was going to protect his baby sister from monsters, super villains, and other common dangers. As he spoke, Conner's eyes dropped from the nurse's eyes to her midsection, which, as it happened, was a nearly perfect globe, a basketball-sized protrusion. She asked more questions, but Conner was no longer listening, transfixed as he was by the sphere under her multicolored hospital scrubs. As his mouth slowly opened, I knew what was coming. And because it was February, I was powerless to stop it.

"When are you having *your* baby?"

The silence that followed was roughly as awkward as you'd expect. The other nurses seated at our table began to study their salads, picking through the lettuce as if they were looking for a lost contact lens. The chatty nurse managed an uncomfortable smile. I didn't exactly help. "Oh, he says that to everyone,"

I laughed, searching desperately for words that would make things better. Instead, I found these: "He would have said the same thing if you looked like a supermodel!"

She furrowed her brow in disbelief, but before she could say anything I gathered the kids—one under each arm, just like in the movies—and whisked them away. Once out of earshot, I tried to impress on them the importance of sensitivity and discretion. "I know you would never deliberately hurt someone's feelings," I said. "But sometimes, Conner, it's better to keep our thoughts to ourselves."

I didn't really blame Conner, though. He was just an innocent kid making an innocent observation. No, I blamed my wife. *Capes?* Who buys their kids capes? None of it would have happened if it hadn't been for the damned capes. And now she was upstairs relaxing comfortably in an adjustable bed, being waited on hand and foot, enjoying all-you-can-eat popsicles and ginger ale, while I was downstairs, by myself, doing the hard work of parenting.

Her intentions were good. The capes were an attempt to get the big kids to buy into the little bundle of joy before they realized just how much time and attention the baby would take from them, which is the central dilemma all parents face when having more than one child. Giving your kid a sibling is the best thing you can do for them, and as often as not, they resent you for it. My wife's ob-gyn told us a story—in the middle of labor—about how he had welcomed his newborn brother to the family by burying him in a basket of dirty clothes and refusing, for hours, to reveal his whereabouts.

Parents will do almost anything to help their kids get along. Very few things bring greater happiness than sibling harmony. But the inverse is also true: There are few things more irritating than listening to children bicker and few things more dispiriting than sibling-on-sibling violence. If war is the failure of diplomacy, then sibling fights feel like the failure of fatherhood.

Sibling rivalry is both eternal and natural. Things ended badly for the very first pair of siblings, Cain and Abel. Why? The usual reason: Because the older kid was jealous of the attention his parents lavished on his baby brother. Siblicide, fittingly referred to as *cainism*, is common among many species of birds and some mammals. Spotted hyenas, for instance, sometimes fight to the death for their mother's attention. Cattle egret hatchlings often do the same, with older and stronger siblings killing younger offspring to ensure their own survival. If things get really tough, they sometimes have them for dinner.

With humans, it usually doesn't go that far. But that hasn't stopped people from studying the heck out of the problem. There are piles and piles of research on virtually every aspect of sibling relationships—sisters and their sisters, brothers and their brothers, sisters and brothers, the importance of birth order, sibling influence, sibling similarities and differences, sibling hatred and love.

And then there's the laymen's stuff. Parenting magazines publish special issues devoted to siblings. Websites provide guides on brother/sister tranquility. Sibling problems are a staple on parenting reality shows like *Nanny 911* and *Supernanny*. The *New York Times* bestseller list includes books like *Siblings without Rivalry: How to Help Your Children Live Together So You Can Live Too.*

At the heart of all of this is a simple question: How do I make my kids get along?

Flip through answers from the self-help world and you wonder whether the "experts" actually have any kids of their own.

Because if so, it sounds like they're raising them not as normal kids but to be the next generation of self-help gurus. So much listening, so much emotion coaching, so much validating.

According to one book by two prominent child psychologists, parents can end fights between their children by channeling negative energy into "some form of creative expression." They suggest that kids be given dolls or pillows and encouraged to release their anger onto those objects, rather than their brothers or sisters. Parents who are especially crafty—in the Michael's, not the Machiavelli, sense—can intervene with "clay, finger paints, or crayon and paper as avenues of expression."

Maybe this works for some families. But in a fight between normal preteen brothers, the crayons are likely to become projectiles, the clay will be used to plug various orifices, and the finger paints just make it harder to figure out who's bleeding.

Where the advice from the professionals isn't absurd, it's obvious: Don't discuss their shortcomings in front of them. Don't dwell on their mistakes and ignore their successes. Don't lavish one child with attention and love and neglect the other. *Really?* You think that might be counterproductive?

So what's the answer? It strikes me as something more than a happy accident that I am extraordinarily close to my three younger siblings even as we approach middle age, and that my own kids—now ages ten, eight, and five—are friends and not enemies. In other words, like everything else in life, it helps to have been born into a good family.

Growing up in suburban Milwaukee, my siblings and I were reasonably certain that we had the strictest parents on the block (which was indisputably true) and that they were ridiculously tough because they *wanted* their kids to be losers (which in hindsight seems less likely). In high school, we had to be home by the time most parties were getting started. When we were visiting friends in that pre–cell–phone era, our folks would actually call ahead to make sure there would be parents at the house, which was unspeakably embarrassing, but not the worst thing they did to us in semipublic. During a holiday break from college one year, my sister, Julianna, stopped at the local video store to rent *The Big Lebowski*. At the cash register, the clerk—a pimply-faced teenager—told my sister that she couldn't rent it because her membership still had a parental block for R-rated movies.

And it wasn't just *what* we could watch, it was *when* we could watch. For as long as I can remember, my parents enforced a complete ban on weekday television. As preschoolers, we didn't protest because we didn't know any better. But I was stunned and disappointed when I learned that my classmates at McKinley Elementary went home and watched *Tom & Jerry* and *The Electric Company*. When I reported this outrage to my younger brother Andy, he sat on the floor, expressionless, in shock. (In fairness, he was just two at the time, so it's possible he didn't fully appreciate the gravity of the situation.)

Over the years, we missed out on an entire generation of classic television: *The Dukes of Hazzard, The Brady Bunch, The Facts of Life, Diff'rent Strokes, Married with Children, The A-Team, Miami Vice*—all of MTV. But it wasn't the shows themselves that we missed. It was that at precisely the time kids are desperate to fit in, we were utterly clueless about the common culture in which our classmates were swimming.

And the abuse didn't stop there. We were subjected to my dad reading James Herriot's *All Creatures Great and Small* in a bizarre Irish brogue that was tinged with Wisconsin—yet at odd times inexplicably morphed into an accent you might expect from a man in New Delhi. But even *that* wasn't the worst. On one drive from Milwaukee to Florida we were confined to the back of our Plymouth Voyager for eighteen straight hours listening to nothing but tapes of Tony Robbins's *Personal Power*.

Yet shared hardship—or even, in our case, a shared imagined hardship—forges strong bonds. We were like fraternity brothers who endure Hell Week together or soldiers who survive boot camp. And with nothing better to do, we spent our childhood years outside, together. There were countless hours of cops and robbers, Wiffle ball, capture the flag, and driveway basketball, along with some now politically incorrect pastimes. Because our elementary school was a block away from home and had a skating rink from November to early March, there was hockey before school, on lunch break, and immediately upon afternoon dismissal.

It wasn't as though we never fought. We did. And there were times I was the kind of mean only an older brother can be. I used to force my siblings to play not-entirely-safe games of basement football: They were the offensive/defensive lines, and I was, always, the heroic tailback vaulting over them into the beanbag end zone. I allowed my sister to opt out of o-line duty to be a cheerleader, if she wanted. (She claims that I once tied her to a pole in the basement and *made* her cheer for us. But I suspect this is apocryphal.)

Injuries were common and sometimes serious. One time I caught Andy with a knee directly to the nose as I went airborne. It was bad. His eyes rolled back in his head and then began to water. Blood washed from his nose in pulsating waves, like water from a rainspout in a storm. "You're fine," I lied. Andy understood he was not fine at all, so I switched tactics. "You know if Mom hears you, we're both dead," I lied again, grabbing a shirt from the dirty laundry to soak up the blood. The poor kid was doing everything he could to quiet his howls of pain. I was helping—okay, maybe "helping"—by stuffing the sleeve of the shirt in his mouth, muffling his cries a bit. It wasn't enough, so I tried something new.

"Awwwww, buddy—I'm really sorry," I said—which was true. Then I laid it on: "Dude, that play was awesome! You were like Ezra Johnson! You stopped me from scoring! That was the greatest play I've ever seen. Seriously, I think you could make the NFL." At which point he began nodding his head in agreement. He was lining up to play again before we'd even stopped the flow of blood.

I shared a bedroom with Andy for virtually all of my childhood. My parents didn't know it at the time, but we stayed up until midnight almost every night. I had a clock radio with a flat, faux-wood top. After we did the dinner dishes we'd race upstairs to listen to whatever sport was on, usually the Milwaukee Brewers or the Bucks. I'd hide the radio under my pillow, and we'd listen and talk and then talk some more.

My sister, Julianna, shared the other bedroom with our youngest brother, Dan, and as we grew bigger the house seemed to grow smaller. I was a sophomore in high school when my folks decided that we needed more space. They expanded our kitchen and added a fourth bedroom. When the work was done, they broke the exciting news in separate meetings—with me first, and then my sister. Because I was the oldest, and because she was the girl, we would each be getting our own bedrooms.

We both refused. The new bedroom stayed vacant.

One of the great ironies of fatherhood is that for most of us it'll be the most important work we do, but there's virtually nothing we can do to prepare for it. There's no way to show up for the first day of the job with any experience. We begin without any idea what we're doing. So it's natural to rely on the example of our own fathers—to emulate our dad if he was a good father and to learn from his mistakes if he wasn't.

There's no such thing as a perfect father, but mine is awfully close. He was firm but never mean, authoritative but never heavy-handed. He worked hard to provide for our family, but his work never seemed to crowd out his time with us. He rarely told us what to do or how to act, but he somehow fostered high expectations. We never feared punishment, but we were afraid of disappointing him. For as long as I can remember, he's drawn comparisons to Atticus Finch. If my kids ever see me the way I see my own dad, I'll consider myself a success. Because he's a big part of the reason Andy, Julianna, Dan, and I are so close.

So I read to our kids in goofy accents and tell bad jokes in front of their friends. I make them attend each others' sporting events, dance recitals, and concerts. They don't watch any television on weekdays. And not long ago I surprised my wife when I asked if she'd be up for spring break in Fiji so that we might "recapture our energy, our focus, and our vitality" at a Life and Wealth Mastery seminar with Tony Robbins. (I kid.)

Hopefully it's rubbing off.

On a recent trip to the supermarket, we pulled into the fire lane to wait while my wife ran in to grab something. The windows were down, and one of the cashiers was on a smoke break. Jane, now five, made clear that she'd internalized our antismoking propaganda. "Yuck, look at that guy smoking," she yelled, easily loud enough for him to hear. "That's disgusting! It's like licking an ashtray!"

The poor guy, just looking for a minute of peace, glanced at the car, stubbed out his butt, and dropped it in the trash before heading back to work.

Conner, who had been watching quietly, shook his head. "I know you would never deliberately hurt someone's feelings, Jane," he said sweetly. "But sometimes it's better to keep our thoughts to ourselves."

CHAPTER 4

Television and Kids
The Beauty and Pain of TV
James Lileks

SHE'S FORGOTTEN VIDEOTAPES. The way the machine grabbed
the plastic slab like an impatient clerk, swallowed it whole,
groaned and whirred as the magnetic heads rose to lick the
tape. The desultory, dentist-drill whine when the tape rewound.
The thrill of fast-forwarding and landing just where you wanted;
the agony of overshooting the scene. The miseries of unlabeled
tapes with inscrutable contents. My child will never know the
guilt a parent feels when they put a tape into the VCR to pla-
cate the kid for a while; you felt like you were shoving a cud of
pre-chewed Lucky Charms—medicated with sedatives—down
her throat.

But you had standards, at least. The tape must be educational. *Busytown* should buy you twenty-six minutes while you
clean the house. You have watched it many times, and you have
made your piece with anthropomorphic, bipedal cats and dogs
whose existence seems oddly centered around explaining the
alphabet and the numbers one through ten. You have learned
not to think too much about Lowly Worm, a limbless creature
in an Alpine hat who is nevertheless capable of operating heavy
machinery and somehow seems to be the moral and ethical
model for Busytown: selfless, industrial, cheerful.

"The author is attempting to rehabilitate the serpent, you
know," you say as you sweep teething-cookie crumbs into a

dustpan. "*Busytown* is obviously a postlapsarian construct in which the symbol of Satan is now reimagined as helpful and self-sacrificing."

Child slurps sippy-cup sauce and nods. Lowly is okay, but *Oh boy here comes Bananas Gorilla! He's funny.* You have a problem with Bananas, an imbecilic simian who provides minor disruptions to Busytown's social order. For one thing, he is identified by his favorite oral pleasure, which suggests he did not choose this sobriquet himself; it's like finding out your college chums called you Cigarette Human when you weren't around. In some episodes he speaks. In some he merely grunts. As a hominid, he is the most advanced creature in Busytown, but he spends his time in criminal pursuits, attempting to procure bananas. Yet he is beloved. *They haven't thought this through.*

So no, not that tape. This one. The one the wife bought at the store. Super educational. *Alphabet Magic* or something. You pop it in the slot—*grab, groan, whine*—and it's cheap computer graphics and a guy who looks like Andy Kaufman playing the emcee from *Cabaret.* He's Alphabet Al. He sings "The Alphabet Song"—but it's not the one that also does duty as "Twinkle, Twinkle Little Star." They composed a new one. He over-enunciates. He mugs. When he gets to Q, you wonder if Q will be for "Quoits," as it was when you were young. The new alphabet song is ingenious, in its own way; you will pick it out on the keyboard later.

You will sing it in the car, later.

You will find it on YouTube, years later, and show it to your daughter, triggering neurons in her almost-teen brain that were ready to consign that memory to cold storage. You will write a piece about Alphabet Al and get an e-mail from someone who knows the actor and sends a link to his punk-rock band. Fourteen years after you put in the tape, you will be driving somewhere with your daughter and for some reason the alphabet comes up, and you sing the Alphabet Al version and *your daughter sings along*. Fourteen years later.

Because of TV. Because of the wonderful, stupid, mass-market, infantile, corporate-loyalty-enhancing, inventive, banal, inspirational, lobotomizing box in the corner.

It's 2001. Daughter has revolved around the sun but once.

It was a time of Teletubbies.

Remember? Bouncy felt-fleshed creatures who ran around and giggled and ate a lot of toast, all under the watchful smile of a flaming baby's head in the sky, until 1940s-style metal speakers emerged from the earth like Orwell's ear trumpet and commanded the Tubbies to rest. Now and then, video entertainment would be displayed on the TV-shaped marks on their bellies, which is a damned inconvenient way to watch a show. Everything would be upside down. The programs shown on their abdominal displays were aimed at children with the mental acuity of cold porridge and seemed inscrutably British. For example: A lady tells stories about a crown. You look over at your child to see if she's showing monarchical sympathies. We fought a war over that, and George Washington didn't die so you could sit here and watch cloth-covered homunculi shove pro-Queen propaganda down your milk-pipe, kid.

"Crown, crown! Where aaaare you?" the lady sang, perhaps channeling centuries of peasants crying out for the king to intercede against the depredations of the nobles. As the lady told the story about the crown to a rapt audience of children, no doubt promised lots of jellied toad or whatever they eat over there, the crown appeared and floated up. The lady told the crown to behave; it did not. Ah: A parable for the dynamic tension between ruled and the ruler, perhaps.

"What a naughty, proud crown," the lady said with toffish disapproval.

I mention this for two reasons. We had a Teletubbies tape, because it wasn't on TV for some reason. This meant that the story of the Naughty, Proud Crown would be repeated daily until the phrase burrowed into our brains like a tick. I would find myself years later dealing with a balky household object like a stuck doorknob in need of oil and say, "What a naughty, proud crown," under my breath. Fast-forward ten years, having a chat with Daughter about the TV of her youth. She had no memory of Teletubbies but had seen them on YouTube and judged them disturbing. I did a search, and the term "naughty proud crown" did not, to my relief, reveal a video of Prince Charles in satirical puppet form applying a riding crop to the buttocks of Camilla Parker-Bowles. No, the first hit was the Tele-tubbies video. Daughter *remembered*.

Fast-forward three years more. Daughter and I are sitting at the kitchen table, waiting for Mom to come home for supper. I thought I heard her downstairs, coming in from the garage. "Mother, Mother, where aaaare you?" I sang.

Wife walks through the door and says, "Crown! Crown! Where aaaaare you?"

Mind you, my wife has never made any pop culture reference of any kind in a quarter century of marriage, and a callback like this stunned Daughter and me.

"What a naughty, proud wife," I said.

"Ewww," said Daughter.

Point is: Those very early TV memories were burned in for the parents, not the child. Because this was our first, our only; because we had just moved to the house of our dreams; because we watched TV with her to gauge her reaction and savor her smiles. And because shortly after we moved, the TV turned into something else, a horrible portal, a window you wanted to paint black.

I have the video of the day it all changed. Jasper Dog is on his back, whining and unnerved. Toddler Daughter in her yellow onesie is smiling up at me, holding a toy telephone that said, "Hello! Hello! Hello!" again and again. Sun on the floor, green leaves outside. On the TV, two tall gray towers ablaze.

In the weeks after 9/11, the nightly TV ration—a little Baby Mozart, a Teletubby show—was the only respite we got from the news. We sat on the sofa with novocained faces watching the naughty, proud crown and the happy goat and the baby-face sun in the sky, and it felt a little bit like watching Mickey Mouse cartoons projected on a bedsheet in a bomb shelter. I dreamed of Tinky-Winky doing the news in Peter Jennings's place.

Daughter, of course, remembers none of it. But she remembers Olie.

Here's the deal with Olie. I can sing the theme, if you like:

> Way up high, in the roly-poly sky?
> There's a little round planet with a really swell guy.
> He's Rolie Polie Olie;
> he's small and smart and round.
> And in the world of curves and curls he's the swellest
>   guy around.
> Howdy. (Howdy!)
> Hooray. (Hooray!)
> And in the world of curves and curls he's the swellest
>   guy around.

I found the show on Playhouse Disney, which was the main morning pacifier. I worked at the kitchen table, laptop plugged into the phone jack on the wall downloading all the horrors, and Toddler Daughter watched her Disney shows on the sofa a few yards away. As I read the news and blogged, she watched four shows, and since the TV was in my line of sight, I watched them, too.

Elmo first. *Thomas the Tank Engine*, which was either a parable of the relations between labor, capital, and the ruling class, all bound together in a system that literally required their interactions to proceed along preordained rails, or a show about self-aware trains. *Dragon Tales*, which was about friendly dragons. The big, strong, male dragon was a lummox; the girl dragon had two heads and was smarter than everyone else. Of course.

Then Olie. She took to this show like nothing else. It concerned a nuclear family of robots—Mom, Dad, Olie, his sister Zowie, and dog Spot. Occasional visits from Uncle Gizmo, who sported an enormous lacquered pompadour, drove a motorcycle, and sounded like Elvis. There was also Pappy, an elderly robot given to by-cracky coot talk, bedeviled by false teeth that sprang from his mouth and ran around the room of their own accord. It looked like it came from a *Marvels of Tomorrow* brochure from the 1939 World's Fair, and the music was straight-up *Little Rascals*–style '30s jazz. It was clever, sweet, funny, and the theme was the signal that the day had really begun. For Christmas the first year in the new house she got plush dolls of all the characters. Spot the dog got a special hug. She said his name. "*SPAH*." She knew him before she saw him.

Eventually new shows came along; she was ten, and Olie was kid stuff. She remembered that she liked him a million years ago, though, so: fire up the Google one night when we're sitting around the table talking, and laugh ourselves to tears over Polish versions of the opening credits.

"Remember Spookie Ookie?" I said.

"He kinda scared me. No, seriously, he did."

And for good reason. The Halloween show on *Rolie Polie Olie* concerned a pumpkin-headed sprite with a malicious grin. When Daughter was young we concluded Halloween with the

Spookie Ookie shows, sitting on the sofa, sifting through piles of candy. It was tradition, until it wasn't. And then I sat on the sofa like a sad dad sack and watched them by myself, because, well, tradition.

There was also a Santa show (Clanky Claus) and an Easter show (Springy Chicken), but they never quite took the same way. The leering face of Spookie Ookie connected with something elemental, an unnerving truth that put the lie to parental reassurances.

Every kid knows there are monsters in the closet, after all, and wonders why Mom and Dad have to pretend there aren't. They know. You can tell by their faces when they look at TV sometimes.

A year ago she says there's a show she likes and thinks I'll get. "It's called *Gravity Falls*. It's just—you have to see it. I can't explain, but it's really cool." And so it is: two smart teenage twins go to spend a summer at a town filled with *X-Files*–style mysteries. Every frame is embedded with things for the Internet obsessives; Greater Mysteries loom in the backstory. In one episode the twins are in a red room that has a zigzag pattern on the floor, and I pause and laugh.

"What?"

"Here." I get out my phone and Google "red room Twin Peaks" and show her: "This is a reference to this." Her eyes shine: secrets. *That is so cool. I wonder if my friends got that. Bet not.* I fire off a tweet about the *Twin Peaks* reference with the proper hashtag and use the Twitter handle for the show's creator. We return to watching. When it's done I check my tweet, and show her a message aimed at me, her dad:

That gum you like is coming back in style

It's a reference to the dialogue spoken by the backward-talking little man in *Twin Peaks*. It's from the creator of *Gravity Falls*.

This is the Most Amazing Moment Ever. This is the Coolest Thing. I can't argue. It's like watching *Star Trek* with my dad, hearing a reference to the USS *Intrepid*, watching Dad call Gene Roddenberry's office to ask if he knew anyone who served on that ship, and getting a letter by registered mail the next day from Gene himself.

Except, of course, I never watched *Star Trek* with my dad. I watched game shows with my mother. She liked *Let's Make a Deal*. My mom wasn't a TV watcher, but she mentioned once that she thought Monty Hall would be the sort of man who was "fun at parties." I think she had a sneaky crush on Monty. I think she imagined sparkling soirees where people stood around in nice clothes, sipping crème de menthe and laughing at the trim Canadian spinning quips. Some nights when Dad had his bowling league we watched Carol Burnett and laughed when Harvey broke up Tim, although sometimes the show—as she put it—"got a little raw." (This meant there were innuendos.) We also watched *Hawaii Five-O* together now and then, and I think she liked Jack Lord, too. Imaginary parties with Jack and Monty trading quips in a suite in a Honolulu hotel, tropical breezes, gay laughter, no one's smoking (everyone on my dad's side smoked and she had to put out the ashtrays and the house reeked for a day and she had to empty a can of Glade), and it's marvelous.

I was completely comfortable watching TV with my mom until suddenly it wasn't cool anymore. So we didn't make popcorn on the stove and put it in the old dented bowls and pour over melted butter, and we didn't laugh at Harvey and Tim together. That was okay, right? Because I was doing other stuff, and your parents can always come up with stuff of their own. I mean, they're grown-ups.

So you're heading off to the Embers with your friend from speech and debate league, and you head downstairs to the furnished basement with its knotty pine and patterned lino-leum and demoted living room furniture and three unloaded rifles on the wall. *Heading out, back by ten.* Your parents are in the recliners, like astronauts in chairs designed to deal with G-forces. Dad has The Remote: the Zenith Space Command. Fargo had four channels. He might push a button once an hour to see what was on, but in those days it was almost an act of civil disobedience to switch networks in the middle of the evening. You made your choice. You committed.

When I got home and found them in the same seats, sports news wrapping up on TV (the local sports personality on Chan-nel 4 wore '70s Herb Tarlek plaids that exploded on the screen in wild, blurry moirés), they would head upstairs, and I'd have the TV to myself. The weekend treats: *Alfred Hitchcock Presents*, and then grainy black-and-white sci-fi. My stuff. Sign-off: The poem about the jet pilot who slipped the surly bonds of earth and touched the face of God, which suggested not enough oxygen was flowing to the mask. Flag. Station ID card. Indian. Static.

TV was a private thing now. It wasn't something we shared anymore. Who in high school watches TV with their *parents*?

"In my time, at the end of the night TV was over." We're driv-ing somewhere, and I've settled into old-timer coot voice. My Pappy Polie voice. Daughter has heard this before.

"*Annnd* you didn't have color, I know, *annnd* you had to watch shows when they were on. I know."

"Exactly. If you missed them, that was it. Maybe they'd be rerun in the summer. All TV in the summer was reruns. Except for the Hudson Brothers or something. Point is I'm used to having what I want to see available whenever I want to see it, and it doesn't seem amazing to me anymore. I pity you. You grew up with this miracle."

"Well, *pardon me* for being born in the twenty-first frickin' century." Mock outrage.

The argument began when we were talking about *The Office*, which we both loved. I watched it on the big TV. She watched it on her phone. I watched it on DVDs. She watched it streamed over the ether. All of her friends were bingeing on the show, and I would hear them chattering in the backseat as I picked them up from soccer. I'd advise them to watch the British version. Uncomfortable silence.

"I tried," one of the friends had said. "It wasn't the same."

"It's excruciating," I said. "And it's British." Something went *ping!* in my head, and I smiled.

British humor. It's the last summer home before I go to college. The local PBS station is running a British comedy show on Sunday nights. My father comes downstairs to get something from his desk, or return a VFW magazine to the bathroom, or possibly just have a few words before his son bolts from the family home, never to return. He watched a few minutes of the comedy show, and I'm sure I radiated spiky teen go-away waves, because he couldn't possibly *get* this.

He sat down. Grabbed the handle of the La-Z-Boy and shifted into full-prone mode. And laughed and laughed and laughed. To my amazement. My father left school in the seventh grade. Built a business out of nothing, spent his days with oil and gas and grease, lost his sense of smell from the constant reek of petrochemicals, hadn't read a book in years as far as I knew, and he's giving himself a side-stitch laughing at *Monty Python*. It was British! It had . . . *references!* And he liked it?

We watched every Sunday that summer, and the most extraordinary thing happened: I shared *Monty Python* references with my father, and still do. A line here, a funny walk there. "Don't mention the war!" he'll say.

"Actually, Dad, that's from *Fawlty Towers*."

"Well, that was a good show, too."

Daughter gave up on TV a long time ago. She hasn't watched a program as it happened for half a decade. She regards Mom as hopelessly recherché, since she watches network TV on the DVR, and even if Mom does find a Netflix show to stream, it's like a 1929 Movietone newsreel about an old lady who wins a Charleston contest. When friends come over, they watch TV, but not like my generation did, slumped and passive. They rewind, freeze, mock, Instagram it, Snapchat a frame with a comment. They live in a media fugue, and there really isn't anything called TV. There's just video, and it's everywhere. There is no sign-off. TV is never over. It is not some Orwellian monoculture blared from inescapable telescreens. In my time we rearranged our lives to fit TV's schedule, and consulted the High Holy *TV Guide* to learn when we should take our places to receive the sermons. Kids today, they press Pause on their computer and pick up the show a day later on their phone.

The end result of ubiquitous access and near-infinite quantity? She watches a tenth of the TV I did at her age. Platforms and channels don't matter. The words "new episode" matter. Watched when you want, where you want, how you want. Hence she may never know the terror of . . . the SPECIAL BULLETIN.

You'd be watching cartoons, or some sitcom, and suddenly the screen would cut to a card that said "SPECIAL BULLE-TIN." "We interrupt this program. . . ." Your heart hit the roof of your mouth so hard your eyes lost focus, because this meant only one thing: toe-to-toe Nu'klr combat with the Rooskies. Cut to the anchorman at a desk, chattering teletypes in the background—and then "Something-something Chou En-lai." Or Nixon trouble. Or whatever. So long as it wasn't *Lakes of Flame Engulfing the World,* you could tell your bladder to cinch it up and stand down.

I hope we never spend a week like 9/11, with the TV always on, the crawl dragging bad news from right to left. But we will. When you're young you fear the world will end all at once. As you age you almost hope it does, at least for yourself: Better the thunderclap-*kaboom* that smotes you fast than the long, drooling decline. The last thing you want to be is the parent reduced to a parenthesis in a room with beeping machinery, your eyes searching for something familiar, your child holding your hand and remembering all the things you lost when your brain got upended like an Etch A Sketch.

It would be apt, though, a neat reversal. Parenthood's beginning is a daily accumulation of details and rituals and songs and books you never forget. Children grow and stretch, rise and mature; their mind, sensing the sedimentary impediment of so many memories, compels them to forget. You remember Lowly Worm and Olie and Mister Noodle and Thomas and Dora and Blue and the rest, just as you remember everything else. They forget most of it, but buried away in their neurons are faces and songs, waiting for the key to turn in the lock.

Speaking of Olie: The department store in 2001 sold Christmas snowglobes with Olie, and his sister, and Spot. It comes out once a year and goes on a shelf for the holidays. I always give it a shake. The snow will settle and rest, of course. But for a while it swirls. I'm not bothered that one day Daughter will inherit it and pack it away. I hope she'll give it a shake and make it come to life, and remember.

Howdy. (Howdy!) Hooray. (Hooray!)

The fireplace, the old dog, the sofa, the crayons, the warm home on a cold day, the chatter of the colorful box in the corner, spinning stories. Everyday life, safe and bright. A short, sweet song we shared.

With occasional pauses for commercials for those Blendy-Pens that let you draw rainbows. And no, I'm not ordering them.

CHAPTER 5

Get Your Kid a Dog
The Moral Case for Pets

Jonah Goldberg

HERE IS WISDOM:

Have a kid? Get a dog.

Want a kid? Get a dog.

Don't want a dog? Get a cat, which is like training wheels for dog ownership.

Have a cat already? It's probably time to get a dog.

Don't like dogs? You're wrong.

Those of you already encumbered with a very small human in your home—and I don't mean Robert Reich—might be asking, "Why?" After all, the humanoid is already making demands on my tolerance for poop disposal and unremunerated feedings. Why would I saddle myself with more and similar obligations—particularly when the four-legged dependent will make demands on me forever and will never carry on the family name or provide me with any kind of tax benefit, or expand the borders of my empire into the barbarian lands of the Gauls?

I can make the practical case. Dogs make good guards, particularly of young children (though this varies by breed; Dachshunds, for instance, are tubular snapping turtles). They are fun to look at and can be entertaining companions. Children raised in households with dogs are less likely to get various immune system–related ailments, such as eczema or asthma. And I suppose if you were starving to death you could consider a canine an emergency reserve supply of protein.

But such arguments fall under the category of rank utilitarianism or instrumentalism. And I want to make a broader case for the beasts, so let me start with first things.

I am a father. I have one child, and let's clear the air right up front: She is better than your child. Maybe not on some test or in a meaningless contest of athletic skill. Certainly if cleanliness is next to godliness, she's a midlist offering, at best. She is better because, as Marines say of their rifles, "This one is mine." She is my greatest concession to relativism. My kid is more important than your kid because . . . well, just *because*. It is an assertion I make in defiance of mere reason and with support of unprovable dogma that runs underneath my feet like veins of granite stretching to the earth's core. I don't begrudge you for disagreeing. In fact, I would think less of you if you didn't. If you told me that you like my kid more than you like your own kid, my first response would be to file for a restraining order.

I bring this up because there is an old notion that keeps reemerging in public life, each time pretending to be something new: the collective ownership of kids. Plato introduced the idea in the *Republic*. Robespierre wanted to create special reform schools—back when the word "reform" had real teeth to it—that would indoctrinate kids into the family of the state. Hitler famously proclaimed, "When an opponent declares, 'I will not come over to your side,' I calmly say, 'Your child belongs to us already. . . . What are you? You will pass on. Your descendants, however, now stand in the new camp. In a short time they will know nothing else but this new community.'" The Soviets lionized kids who turned in their parents for disloyalty, which, in Soviet life, meant that the parents were holding back food and, instead of giving it to the state, were using it to feed their family.

Back in the sexist days when totalitarianism was always masculine, these sentiments were couched in stern, patriarchal terms. Now that we're more enlightened, the same idea has been repackaged as a mommy thing. "We have to break through our kind of private idea that kids belong to their parents or kids belong to their families," Wake Forest professor Melissa Harris-Perry cooed on MSNBC a couple years ago. More than a decade before that, Hillary Clinton insisted that "as adults we have to start thinking and believing that there isn't really any such thing as someone else's child."

It's my view that we have a Second Amendment largely to make sure that no one makes the mistake of thinking that my kid is their kid. But one needn't be so strident. One can simply argue on empirical grounds that this is a really stupid idea. The simple fact is that before we are citizens or Americans or anything like that, we are humans (you could look it up). It was Kant who said, "Out of the crooked timber of humanity, no straight thing was ever made."

And if there's any truth to that, surely you can't organize a healthy civilization around the idea that large numbers of people can be made to care about an abstraction—"the children"—as much as they care about the very real and manifest creature that is their own child. This is a variant of Friedrich Hayek's "knowledge problem." Just as a widget manufacturer must have a superior ability to set prices for his widgets rather than a bureaucrat in Washington, so too must a parent—speaking generally—have superior ability to decide what is best for his kid. "My educational policies are based on the fact that I care more about my children than you do," Phil Gramm famously explained to a woman. She shot back, "No, you don't." To which Gramm replied, "Okay, what are their names?"

This is a long way around the barn on our way to dogs, but bear with me (which is what Tonto would say by way of explanation if he had an ursine *kemosabe*). Without naming names, a certain editor baited me into writing this chapter by revealing himself to be an evil monster when he told me—this is a direct quote—"I hate dogs."

Where to begin? Let's start by stipulating that dogs are not children. Yet they are members of the family. Before I get to the metaphysics of this distinction, I will simply note that it is true as a matter of popular opinion. According to Pew, 85 percent of dog owners consider their dog part of the family. Ninety-four percent of dog owners say they feel "close" with their dog—which is quite a lot, considering that only 87 percent report feeling close with their mother and 74 percent with their father. A 2011 survey found that 54 percent of pet owners consider themselves "pet parents" rather than "pet owners." More than two-thirds of these pet parents get their animals birthday and Christmas presents. For reasons that defy rational analysis, many of them wrap the gifts, too.

Of course, public opinion is not dispositive of anything except the opinion of the public. If political philosophy teaches us anything—an open question, by the way—it is that "the people" can be wrong. But evolution and psychology are also on my side. The dog stands alone in the animal kingdom. Of all of God's creatures, it is the only one that clearly chooses to cast its lot with humanity. For complicated reasons lost to prehistory, humans and some lupine dog precursor worked out a businesslike arrangement where they each helped out the other. In the evening, dogs would do some light security work, and during the day they'd pitch in when shopping for woolly mammoths and antelope. Humans would share the bones and the campfire. Like many relationships that start out as just business, friendships were formed. Over the millennia, those friendships soaked into our DNA as a bond of love.

Not everyone is on board, of course. Evolutionary absolutists and other secular buzzkillers concede these broader facts of the human-Fido compact, but disagree about the "love" stuff.

They claim that dogs are really "social parasites" who've evolved clever techniques for separating naked apes from bacon and kibble. "Dogs belong to that elite group of con artists at the very pinnacle of their profession," writes historian and science writer Stephen Budiansky, "the ones who pick our pockets clean and leave us smiling about it."

The problem with this interpretation (other than its utter joylessness) is that it is completely wrong. Sure, one can employ a crude reductionism that says dogs act like they love us because their genes tell them to, and vice versa. But so what? You can apply the same crude reductionism to children and wives. That doesn't mean I don't love *them*. To say that love is some evolutionary con is to suggest that some other real motive lurks behind the Potemkin façade of the con artist. But there's simply no evidence of this. I've watched my dogs closely over the years. When I've given them a bone, they did walk away with it—almost invariably to the cleanest corner of my most expensive rug—but they didn't walk away snickering and calling me a sucker. When I come home to Zoë, my Carolina dog (aka an "American Dingo"), she is not pretending to be happy to see me any more than I am pretending to be happy to see her. The joy you see is the joy you feel.

There's an old joke, now immortalized in forwarded e-mails from strangers, that goes something like this: There's a simple test for figuring out who loves you more, your dog or your wife. Lock them both in the trunk of your car for six hours. When you open it, note which one is more happy to see you.

In the year 2000, my then-fiancé and I rescued Cosmo, who would—thanks solely to my shameless pimping at National Review Online—become known to some as "the It dog of the American right." Cosmo was our trial-run baby. And I mean that quite seriously. Dogs aren't as much of a responsibility as a human child, but they are the closest we can get (at least until the Japanese work out some kinks in their robotics). You can leave a cat alone in your house for days as long as there's enough food left out. And when you return, they'll barely notice. But dogs require active ownership. And truth be told, *ownership* is probably the wrong word for it. It may seem like a sign of civilizational rot to say it, but parenting is closer to the reality of canine stewardship than ownership. One owns a car; one doesn't merely "own" a dog. Because the dog also owns you.

To bring this back to where we started, dogs are an antidote to all forms of totalitarian thinking. Our connection to them cannot be politicized. Children should not be politicized either, but as future citizens, voters, workers, taxpayers, and economic cogs, they are simply too tempting a target for the politicians, planners, and meddlers. Moreover, it's impossible as a parent not to worry about how the polis deals with your child and how your child deals with the polis. I really don't care what kind of music my dog listens to. I have never rushed to change the channel when she trots into the room. Children, however, are different. Being a good parent requires caring about politics, teaching them about the polis. Dogs keep their innocent doggy goodness from kennel to grave, obviating the need to explain to them why, for instance, certain politicians are good and others are reprehensible. Yet this blessed doggy innocence can be wonderfully helpful in the moral and philosophical formation of your children.

Dogs serve as a reminder that some bonds are stronger and more deeply felt than those that can be described by politics or the ephemeral pieties of a given moment. They live inside a moral universe defined solely by the pack or, if you prefer, the family.

Dogs inculcate a sense of rightly-ordered priorities. If I've learned anything living in Washington, it's that politics is relevant only to limited and specific parts of our individual and collective lives. Inside the microcosm of the family, we're all socialists. We do not monetize our love for our children, and we do not present our kids with a bill for room and board (at least not until they're grown and move into our basements). Our most important obligations are prior to mere economic, political, or even most religious considerations. (God did ask Abraham to sacrifice Isaac, but barring an explicit and personal request from the Almighty, few of us would put religion ahead of our children's well-being. Thank God—literally—such requests are vanishingly rare these days.)

And dogs teach you an awful lot about life. They're a lot of work. And the trauma of losing a dog is one of those cruel realities that can be hard to impose on a child at an early age. But that's the point. Life happens, and children need to learn about it eventually. But in the process, they also learn what it means to take some share of responsibility for another life. They learn that the real joys are small and personal. They learn that there are many dogs in the world, but this one is ours and we are hers. The thin veneer of activity we call civilization and all that it entails is a macrocosm outside of the microcosm of love. The macrocosm is larger and so much more important in countless objective ways, but the microcosm takes up more room in our hearts and matters so much more to our souls. One must obey the rules of the macrocosm. But the first law of the microcosm is that our love is greater, more real, and more enduring than anything that can be quantified by mere reason. There's an awful lot of moral instruction you can give a kid in the form of a puppy.

And finally, there's politics: There are no Democratic dogs, no Republican hounds.

Years ago, my wife returned from the dog park, crestfallen, with Cosmo waggling happily by her side. The Wonderdog, as we sometimes called him, had betrayed her profoundly. "What did he do?" I asked, immediately taking his side, at least a little.

"A fat man got out of a van with a bunch of dogs, and Cosmo ran up to him and was all buddy-buddy with the fat man. He let him pet him."

"So what?" I asked.

"The fat man was Ted Kennedy."

"Oh, Cosmo," I said shaken.

But forgiveness came quickly as Cosmo sat down on my wife's feet and asked for a scratch behind his ear.

CHAPTER 6

In Praise of Adventure

*How to Fill a Child's Life with Excitement and
Danger (Without Getting Them Killed)*

Tucker Carlson

I'VE HEARD people say that they never really felt like adults until their parents died. That makes sense, but it's not how I made my final break with childhood. Mine came while walking through Walmart not long after my thirty-fifth birthday. I'd come to buy a trash can but somehow found myself in the sporting goods aisle, standing in front of the largest display of BB guns I'd ever seen. There were Daisy Red Ryders and scoped Beeman target rifles, CO_2-powered pellet pistols and something called the Gamo Buckmaster Squirrel Terminator. I counted at least a dozen Crosman 760 Pumpmasters, a weapon regarded by every boy in my sixth-grade class as the AK-47 of air rifles for its power and durability.

For a full minute I stared. *Man, I wish I could get one of those,* I thought.

Then it dawned on me: I'm a grown man with a valid driver's license. I can buy as many BB guns as I want.

So I did.

In the end I bought one of each. On my way to the checkout counter, I spotted a shelf of blowguns. They were four feet long and made of machined, aircraft-grade aluminum, each with a quiver of steel knitting needles for darts. "Deadly accurate at ranges of more than 20 yards," the package promised. I bought a pair of them. Then I drove home and gave the entire arsenal to my kids to play with. In my house, we believe in dangerous toys.

It's a faith I inherited. One of my earliest and most vivid memories starts on a dirt road in Southern California early in the Carter presidency. I'm seven, my brother is five. We are lying facedown on the roof of our family's 1976 Ford Country Squire station wagon, a wood-paneled land yacht almost nineteen feet long. My father is in the driver's seat smoking a Pall Mall. "Hold on," he yells through the open window. My brother and I grip the leading edge of the luggage rack, splaying our legs like snipers. My father guns the massive V8, and we shoot forward at high speed over culverts and potholes and rocks. At one especially steep hump in the road we seem to catch air, and I look over in time to see my brother in flight, tethered to the vehicle only by his fingertips. His mouth is opened wider than I have ever seen it. He is screaming with happiness.

I've sometimes wondered what car surfing was meant to teach us. My father had a reckless streak, but he was kind and always deliberate. Every activity came with a message about deeper truths. Was he trying to instill in us a proper sense of fatalism, the acknowledgment that there is only so much in life you can control? Or was it a lesson about the importance of risk? "Who dares, wins," he often said, quoting the motto of the Special Air Service. Until you're willing to ride the roof of a speeding station wagon, in other words, you're probably not going to leave your mark on the world.

That's all wise advice, if seldom heard anymore, and I've done my best to pass it on to my own four children. But I suspect there was another motive at work. My father loved dangerous toys because dangerous toys are the most interesting kind. Sure, it's momentarily entertaining to watch a Slinky walk down stairs, but spend an afternoon playing with lawn darts, and you're apt to learn an enduring lesson. Dangerous toys are an education. By that measure, my brother and I were the most erudite kids in the neighborhood.

One of the first things we learned was that shopping carts aren't built for speed. We'd liberated one from a nearby super-market and decided to race it down the hill in front of our house. Since he was younger and less aware of consequences, my brother climbed into the basket and took the first ride. Within ten feet, all four wheels turned sideways and he wound up with a bloody nose and gravel in both palms. After that we stuck to mopeds, scooters, and riding our skateboards while holding car bumpers.

Shortly after my sixteenth birthday, my father decided it was time for me to learn to drive a car. He gave me the first lesson himself, in a movie theater parking lot. Then he rented me a car for a month and wished me luck. It was a white Chrysler with an AM radio and a manual transmission. I drove it all over San Diego, leaving clouds of melted clutch smoke at intersections.

After a while it seemed prudent to get a driver's license. There was a written test and a driving exam, but before taking either I had to spend a week at a state-approved driver's edu-cation course. It was held in a strip mall, six hours a day, and it was deadly boring. Classes consisted mostly of lectures on speed limits and unintentionally hilarious DUI videos. I drove myself to and from school every day.

By Thursday, this had caught the attention of the kid sitting next to me, a droopy-eyed stoner with a blond butt cut and a puka shell necklace. During lunch break, he confronted me. "Wait a minute, dude," he said, obviously baffled. "We're in driving class so we can get a drivers license to drive. But you drove here. How'd you do that?"

Good question. My father laughed when I told him about it.

My father was famous among our friends for his sense of humor and for letting us do perilous things with vehicles. But the most dangerous thing he let us do was root around unsupervised in his library, which was vast and eclectic. He had books on virtually everything interesting and weird, from accounts of cannibalism in Micronesia to transcripts of court-martials from the Boer War. He had an especially large collection of extremist literature he'd picked up as a reporter while covering the lunacy of San Francisco in the 1960s. I'll never forget the day we came across *The Anarchist Cookbook*. It was on a high shelf next to *The Poor Man's James Bond*.

Both books have since been the subject of court cases, and it's easy to see why. Not only do they endorse the violent overthrow of the existing order, they offer detailed instructions on how to achieve it using common household items. Within days my brother and I had constructed a remarkably effective flamethrower.

From there we moved to ordnance. After school one day we built improvised hand grenades using hydrochloric acid we'd bought for $1.50 a gallon in the pool cleaning section of the hardware store. It was a simple recipe: Pour half a pint into a glass bottle, add some bits of aluminum foil, cap tightly, and get away fast. They went off like a 12-gauge, leaving a satisfying cloud of chlorine gas. We spent many happy hours lobbing them onto the golf course near our house.

There may have been such a thing as travel soccer when I was a kid, but I never heard of it. Nor did we ever seem to have much homework. What we did have was lots of free time, and we spent most of it in martial pursuits. We made nunchucks out of broom handles and throwing stars from circular saw blades. We staged elaborate bottle-rocket wars and had pellet-gun skirmishes in the backyard. (In a misguided nod to safety, my brother insisted we wear glass diving masks for eye protection.) We constructed a pair of enormous slingshots from rubber surgical tubing and fired water balloons at each other. We played Mumblety-peg with kitchen knives and screwdrivers.

Sometimes, when we were feeling ambitious, we took the trolley to Tijuana. After decades of being invaded by Marines on leave from Camp Pendleton, downtown Tijuana was an open–air vice mall, though relatively safe as long as you didn't argue with anybody. In 1981, there was nothing evil you couldn't find there. For the older kids, the lure was tequila and hookers and the countless unregulated pharmacies that sold codeine-based cough syrup and over-the-counter Percocet. For us, it was all about the switchblades and fireworks. Especially the fireworks.

Tijuana firecrackers were the size of Twinkies. Made from rolled newspaper and sulfurous gunpowder and painted red, they were like sticks of dynamite from a Roadrunner cartoon. And you could buy them by the pound in plastic grocery bags. Every bag identified them as "M-80s," but we knew better. Quality control was an abstract concept in pre-NAFTA Mexico, so each firecracker promised an exciting new surprise. Some sputtered harmlessly, while others left craters in the lawn. Some did both, posing as duds until you walked over to them, at which point they exploded, leaving you deaf for the day.

One afternoon I headed to a friend's house to field-test a new batch of explosives. He lived more than a mile away, mostly uphill, so instead of riding my bike I decided to take the go-kart my brother and I had gotten for Christmas. I don't know where my father bought it, but the machine looked homemade, with a plumbing pipe frame, lawnmower engine, and no muffler. It rode just a few inches off the pavement. You could hear it three streets over.

I made it out of our neighborhood to the main intersection in town, where I waited in traffic for the stoplight to change. As I idled there thinking about firecrackers, I noticed people in the cars around me staring down at the go-kart. They looked slightly alarmed, but nobody said anything. The light changed, and I drove off with my sack of M-80s. Later that day I drove home. It was a different country then.

By the time my own children were born, there were no more go-karts on city streets. America's moms were firmly in charge, and that meant safety was a virtue for its own sake, a concept that had never occurred to me growing up. There wasn't much I could do about it. You might not like a cultural consensus, but bucking it is fruitless, if not illegal. At the very least it exposes you as a crank.

So I made do with low-grade subversion. My father helped by regularly giving the kids shotguns and Maasai war spears for Christmas. I did my part by letting them steer the car while sitting on my lap, which of course they loved. That continued until I bought a new car and discovered that its airbags could be fatal to small children. "Pretty ironic," I huffed to my mechanic, "that a device designed to protect us might wind up killing my kids." He looked at me blankly and flat-out refused when I asked him to disconnect them. "Airbags are mandatory," he said. "It's the law." There's no fighting the Mommy State.

Except possibly with potato cannons. That was my hope when I bought them, anyway. A potato cannon is a length of plastic drain pipe, capped at one end, with a barbecue igniter set in the back as a trigger. Filled with a flammable aerosol, like hairspray or underarm deodorant, it becomes the homeowner's RPG. It will fire a potato the span of a football field and through a sheetrock wall. It also shoots limes and peaches and apples and chunks of ice. And since I live in a house with three daughters, it was only a matter of time before we loaded the thing with Barbies.

It happened after lunch in late August one year, on one of those sweltering days that make you want to do something wrong. Out of the blue my son suggested firing a Barbie doll out of the cannon, which struck me as inspired. So, over his sisters' objections, we did.

The result was an epiphany. I wasn't there when scientists mixed chocolate with peanut butter to produce the world's first Reese's cup, but the moment had that same feeling of harmonic convergence. The doll left the muzzle with her hair on fire and continued to blaze like a plastic meteor all the way over the house onto the front lawn. Even my daughters were in awe.

Soon there was a crowd of neighborhood kids in our yard waiting for me to do it again. I took the opportunity to tell them the following story, which, by the way, was pretty much true:

"A few years ago in Texas," I said, "a couple of boys loaded a potato cannon with a live bullfrog. Everything went fine until one of the boys decided to peer down the muzzle. You can guess what happened next. The gun went off. One of the boys wound up blind. Doctors are still picking pieces of frog out of his face."

The kids listened slack-jawed to the tale, which was both a reminder to be cautious around guns and a warning against cruelty to animals. Parable delivered, I prepared to blast another Barbie over the roof. "Ready! Aim! Fire!" the kids chanted. I hit the igniter. Nothing happened. I hit it again. Silence.

That's when I did something I still regret, and my kids still talk about. I unscrewed the back of the gun, stuck my face close to the combustion chamber, and unaccountably pressed the igniter.

The fireball that emerged vaporized most of the hair above my shoulders, including my eyelashes, eyebrows, and everything else back to the top of my head. I looked freakish. Like a clown, or Liza Minnelli's fourth husband. My wife was horrified—and, worse, vindicated. But at least the kids learned something.

CHAPTER 7

Catechesis

Teaching Your Kid about God

Larry Miller

Ooh! Remember your first kiss? Remember your game-winning homer in Little League? Remember when Ann, the super-sweet and super-pretty blonde cheerleader, was so nervous reading her paper in tenth-grade English she didn't know her skirt had hiked up, showing her undies in front, and your teacher, Miss Cesario, had to tip-toe up and quietly tell her, which made all the boys, including you, *furious*?

Yes, you do. Of course you do.

Here's another! Remember Dad teaching you how to light a barbecue, which got a little out of hand and kind of exploded? Remember Mom storming outside, shooting Dad a look from the Dark Ages, and telling you, as she dragged you back inside by the ear, that it was positively the last barbecue-lighting you were going to witness for the rest of your life (although you kept sneaking out for them)? Remember how good the burgers were, even though you were pretty sure the weird taste around the edges was lighter fluid?

Yes, you do. Of course you do.

All right! We're all warmed up! How about this one!

Remember your first prayer? Remember Dad teaching you to look around church or temple each time to let it sink in: "This is a good place, a holy place"? Or the time you really began to think you didn't just believe in God, you knew Him?

No, you don't. Of course you don't.

Shouldn't prayer cancel out all other memories? (Except for Ann's underwear; I mean, come on.) But most of you still don't know. Did Dad teach you to pray? Have you taught your own children? Breath out, calm down, come with me, and we'll find out together.

I have good memories of my temple in childhood. It wasn't built yet when we moved out to Long Island from Brooklyn when I was three, but all the other new families were just like us, and my parents joined immediately and signed up for every way they could help as soon as we got there: planning, building, cleaning, committees, furniture, everything.

So I guess you could say there was a congregation before there was a temple, and everyone chipped in and bought a small house and we used that. All the services and classes were held in that house while the regular place was being built, and all the members participated. Crowded, but so what? I liked that little house. I can still see the handfuls of students in the tiny bedroom classes and the writing on the blackboards, and hear the stories and the liturgy.

The whole neighborhood was new itself and still being built, and the trees were thin and little, but so were we. I guess I didn't know much at the time, but it seemed to me it was just the right place to build a temple as we were building ourselves.

I made a lot of friends there, and we learned everything together. We played a lot of ball; we all started looking at the girls like, well, girls, at the same time; and we all pitched in, too, fixing and storing and carrying. This kept going long after the temple was finished, with bar mitzvahs and classes, and Kiddush after Saturday services where I first learned to love herring. And it went all the way up to me valeting cars at all the weddings for several years before I went to college. That's right, I said several years. Guests used to laugh when I brought their cars around and shout, "Look at this one! He doesn't even look old enough to have a license!"

That was more correct than they would want. I didn't look old enough because I wasn't. None of us had licenses. Whenever a guest in a suit and his wife in a gown pulled up to an affair in a car with a stick shift and went upstairs smiling and waving, we would all wave back and then instantly run to call up every other carboy who wasn't working that day, and we'd all ride our bikes to the temple and learn how to drive a stick. Sometimes it was a Nomad wagon with three on the tree, and sometimes it was a Corvette with four on the floor, but it made no difference to us. The guests didn't notice their cars had fifteen extra miles on them when they came out flush from the big party, and the caterer never said anything. (I think God will mention it, though, at our Big Meeting someday. I think He'll want me to explain just one more time how driving a "borrowed" car wasn't stealing. Ah, well.)

We did so much in that temple. Every time there was a war on Israel, we would all get together in the sanctuary and pray, and then raise money for an ambulance, or medical or military supplies, right there, and the rabbi would pass the news on to us from the pulpit. You know, folks, this was years before any place like CNN or Fox News, and I remember how close we all felt to get the news together. Who was wounded, who was missing, who was killed—news has never felt that real since. I think I'd like to experience news that way again, with everyone all together.

I learned to pray at that temple from my father, and that's the point. He's the one who taught me. The best lesson was always being at services with Dad. He and Mom are passed on now almost twenty years. Every Saturday I would go early with Dad, and we would plop ourselves down as close to the front as we could get, and when my mom and sister would join us later, I'd get up and move to the back or stand along the wall.

Here's another reason it was special, though. Dad was self-taught. He never grew up knowing Hebrew or ritual, but a lot of my mom's relatives wore black hats, and Dad started teaching himself, which is actually kind of amazing. It's not an easy language, but he learned everything. Sure, his pronunciation was off and he wasn't very rhythmic, but I loved hearing him, and he wanted my mother to see, and he wanted my sister to see, and he wanted our neighbors to see, and he wanted God to see.

There was an extra-special reason, too: He wanted *me* to see. No one had taught him, and he wanted to teach me. He wanted his son to respect him for praying well and knowing what to do, and I did. He wanted to be a father who taught his son.

Showing your children what you look like with prayer on your lips and building a home that reflects your beliefs are very important things to do. This is how you teach.

If there's a God (and, by the way, there is) He probably won't care how many card tricks you taught Junior, but He might care quite a bit what you taught your kids about Him. Your kids will learn how to teach their kids and—who knows?—many years from now you might just get a nice, comfy cloud thrown in up there from God.

Pop prayed with his heart, but everyone in temple always knew he was there, because there was one tiny problem: He was completely tone deaf and couldn't sing a lick.

I'm telling you, folks, not a lick. Nothing wrong with that, and he wasn't shy and loved to sing out with the congregation, but at the end of the day—and at the beginning, and in the middle, too—I'll bet he never hit one note right, not even close. How bad? Sharp blasts of a foghorn across lonely midnight water would sound nicer to you than Dad praying.

One of our famous family stories was how Daddy, the sweetest man I ever knew, saw the singer Vaughan Monroe in a restaurant, got up from our table, knelt down behind Mr. Monroe with a big smile, and sang the first few bars of "Racing with the Moon." Monroe turned to my father and said, "You make me feel very secure."

Yes, Dad taught me to pray. He taught himself, and then he taught me.

He taught me how to see and feel the synagogue. He taught me that you can always talk to God, but in temple He's much closer, so you don't have to shout.

Dad didn't have a good voice, but he'd always say, "God hears me, and He knows what I'm saying, and that's all that matters. Just make sure He hears you, too." Then he'd always smile. Always.

So listen up, all you red-blooded guys. You want to teach your kids manners and study habits and how to hit a curve? Fine, but these things mean nothing—*nothing*—if you forget your first job. And your first job is to teach them how to pray. "Make sure He hears you, too." Let your little boy see you close your eyes and speak to God, and let him know you mean it. Teach him that your church or temple is not a candy store or a sneaker shop. Teach him to understand what's holy. Teach him to stop before entering the sanctuary and think, *This is God's house. We built it, but it's God's. We printed these prayer books, but they are God's. When we sing, it's really God's voice, not ours. We come here to listen, but God comes here to speak. These walls are like the insides of a fine violin: They've absorbed much over the years, but they are still shiny and smooth and waiting for you.*

Hey, don't fidget. There's a lot more to—all right, fine, if you have to pee, make it fast and come back, because teaching the kids to pray was just your first job, and you have three of them.

Now it's time for number two, and here it is: They know how to pray, *but they don't know where.*

You can watch baseball on TV, but think about how much better it is to go to the stadium with your kids, walk through the tunnel into the sunlight, look at that green field, and watch their faces light up.

Every place is good for a prayer, and everything good is worth a prayer.

Seeing your new baby for the first time, or nine months before when you made that baby, or at a Pop Warner game when your kid's playing hard, or getting to the bathroom at the train station just in time? (And I do mean *just in time.*) Say one there. No better time for a glance heavenward and a thank-you.

Everything, everywhere. You and your wife have been planning to go out to dinner for a long time, right? Just the two of you, and you can't seem to get it done. You're tired, or working, or the kids have a game, and the one night you and she finally plan ahead and get a sitter. . . . Well, you kiss the kids goodnight, drive to a quiet place down the block for a meal, an hour and a half alone, and the waiter puts two cocktails down in front of you? Good Lord, folks, isn't that a fine moment to look at each other, smile, clink glasses, and then look up and raise your glasses again, and say "Thank you" to the guy who gave it all to you, the One who's really watching the kids? Can anyone not see that?

Sitting at your desk, walking along a city street, snoozing on a park bench on a sunny day, perched on a stool at the counter of a good diner when the cook puts a big plate of breakfast down in front of you, noticing a scantily clad girl in a bar and seeing her wink at you as you dash over to beat the rush? (Just kidding about the girl in the bar. I wanted to see if you were still listening. Besides, God understands these things. I think.)

Yes, pray everywhere, and they don't have to be long ones, and not just for you. If an ambulance roars past with the siren on, say one for the guy they're saving. If someone in rags is picking things out of a garbage can, say one for him. If high school kids are strolling by laughing and happy, say one for them. These are all good places.

But not the best places. Let's start with the ones in all the books. They're not the best, but they're close. The kind even God sees and says, "Wow."

For instance, if you're Catholic, I would think going to St. Patrick's in New York would be very moving, or the Cathedral of Notre Dame in Paris, or St. Peter's, or the Hagia Sophia, or hundreds of others that will take your breath away. Not just the huge and artistic ones, either. There are thousands of humble, brick-and-mortar churches in small towns and on country roads with a sun-worn priest in each, all waiting for you to stick your head in and sit down.

If you're one of the many denominations of Protestants, there are so many magnificent churches across America and internationally, and you'll never go wrong visiting St. Paul's in London (or anything else with Christopher Wren's name on it). Again, though, I think the simple churches on town squares and country roads with their white, wooden towers have the greatest pastors, and real warmth and light. God loves the fancy ones, but I think He has an extra-special place for these.

If you're Jewish, go to Israel. It's that simple.

There are many religions we're not getting to, and I'm sure they have fine places, too.

Now forget about them. All of them. Forget who they're named after, forget where they are, forget who the guest speaker is, forget the gold or the cinderblocks or the feathered fans.

Think of one thing: You. Yourself. Your church, your temple. Your family. Your seat. Your prayer. You've been a member there for more than long enough. It's yours. That seat is your property, yes, but you are that seat's property, too. The seat belongs to you, but you belong to it, and think about this: You belong to that sanctuary just as it belongs to you. You belong to that prayer.

Think of all the people who were in that seat before you, and say "Thank you" to them and wish them well wherever they are. Tell them you're happy to be part of the group. Tell them you will say a good prayer.

Look down at yourself and be grateful you took the time to shower and put on good clothes. Your seat and your God deserve to see you at your best. Look around the sanctuary and feel what a good room they have made. Say how glad you are to be there. You're not the only one. God approves of it, and He approves of all those who've tried so hard in that seat. He knows them all deeply and has watched them and judged them. So be humble, but be grateful out loud for being allowed to come to such a holy place.

The whole place is the same in there. The pulpit belongs to you, and you belong to it. The walls and the banners and the priests and the ministers and the rabbis. You own them, and they own you. Acknowledge it and say "Thank you."

Thank God. Thank Him again and again for your health and the health of those you love. Thank Him for those you love who are with Him in heaven, and thank Him for making that love real forever, because it is. Those souls, your parents and loved ones, are watching you and smiling, too. Smile back and tell them you love them. They are as real as you are.

This is all a very good way to start a prayer. Don't feel guilty or silly that you're not concentrating, because you are. Stand and sit and pray with the congregation, but with every other second, pray and think and smile and be grateful. Practice makes perfect, and you won't be perfect, because no one is, but the more you pray in that seat, the better it gets, and these thoughts and prayers on your own are the perfect way to begin. And you know what? That's a big part of how to pray. Which brings us to the *why*.

Here's the important part: It's all about God, but then again, maybe it's not. Not all. There's a reason God made the world and made us. He's perfect, but He wanted more. He wanted someone to watch. He wanted family. So He created more. He created us. We are the more. God not only wants our hearts and souls to be right, He needs them to be. It's all about God, yes, but that one tiny fraction left? That's us, and that's the way He meant it to be. We need to pass and succeed, but here's something you probably don't know: He needs us to pass the tests and be good enough to get to Him. One without the other is not complete.

God is everything, but we are the magic dust that makes it come to life.

That's the start of how you know Him.

Give in, give up, and believe. It's far easier than you think. Say what's in your heart and don't be afraid you're going to look stupid. Here's a big secret: You know who looks stupid right now? *You.* You won't look stupid when you pray, but even if you do, hey, you're already praying, so who's going to say anything?

You were shy before you asked your wife out on a date when you met. So what? Now you're married and have kids. You were shy when you went on a job interview. So what? Now you work there and make a good living for your family.

You get the point. Don't be shy talking to God. Tell Him the truth, since He knows it anyway. Tell Him you're afraid, you're worried, you're happy, you're sad—tell Him everything that's in your heart. Stand up, look up, and reach up. Then tell Him you want to be part of His team. Remember, He knows everything. He's just waiting for you to try, and He's already smiling with His arms out for a hug.

He's right there. Where? There. Right in front of you. You

will feel something the second you do it. One tingle grows into two. You may not see anything or feel anything. Again: So what? Maybe you'll feel something the next time. But you do feel something! You feel great that you tried. And you'll never be afraid to do it again.

That's the most important part. You didn't know if you believed before you prayed? What are you talking about? You just told Him your greatest desires. You just spoke out loud and were honest. You just smiled and looked out and said, "Thank you."

Guess what? You believe. Don't be afraid. You believe. Just a little to start, but that grows, and you'll know it every day. You didn't love your wife the first time you saw her, but that grew, and now you do. God is much the same way.

All you have to do is want to. All you have to do is try.

It's exciting, though. You don't know what you're doing? Yes, you do. You're open to Him. You're waiting for Him. And it's going two ways! He's waiting for you, too! You're way past belief. You chatted. You did it. You not only believe . . .

You know. You know Him. You know God. Yes, you do. God knows every single thing about you, doesn't He? Of course He does. And you know every single thing about Him, don't you? Sure you do. There's an old, big book you have in your house, or you can pick it up in any bookstore. It's a Good Book, and it's waiting for you.

That book is also in every hotel room in America. You know that book. You know the start of your belief. Say hello in front of your mirror when you're getting dressed and ask for help. Say hello when you're watching the sun set and give thanks.

Here's something amazing: The greatest, most godly men and women in history were just like you, and they were afraid, too, but now that you've reached out and tried, you're just like them.

So. Where are we? Right where we started? Oh, no. You know how to start praying, and you know how to pray, and you know how much is waiting for you. Good.

You know how to find the great places in the world to pray, and you know how every simple place is great, too. But now you know about the cherry on top. You know how to sit down in your own church or temple and begin. You know that seat is the greatest place in the world to pray. It's yours now. Good. Plus, you know there's a God waiting for you. You know He's listening. You know Him.

You know how, you know where, and you know who. So teach yourself. And teach your children.

If your parents have passed away, they're in heaven. Think about them, and talk to them, and remember. I'm looking forward to seeing them. That's where it all starts.

Remember: Make sure He hears you, too.

Mom? My mom's love flowed through our house like Niagara Falls. She scrubbed us and taught us to behave and was so smart she seemed to know everything. I loved her then, and I love her now. But Dad?

Oh, my daddy. He always sang "The Star-Spangled Banner" at ball games, loved dogs as much as they loved him, and he always had a big smile when coming in the door after a hard day's work. But how I wish I could hear that good man pray again.

CHAPTER 8

Surviving School
It's Just as Bad the Second Time Around

Joe Queenan

AFTER THEIR CHILDREN are all grown up and have moved away for good, parents are supposed to suffer from profound melancholy and sometimes even outright depression. This is the phenomenon widely known by the horrid little term "empty-nest syndrome."

It all went by too fast; we didn't really enjoy those precious little moments as much as we should have; the future now looks so bleak, rueful empty nesters say to themselves, nostalgic for the glorious, halcyon days when their children were young and innocent and still nesting.

Or so runs the popular mythology.

This has not been my experience as a parent. From the moment my children left home forever, I felt a radiant, ineffable joy suffuse my very being. Far from being depressed or sad, I was elated. There was a simple reason for this: From that point onward, I would never again have to think about the kids and school. Never, ever, ever. I would never have to go to the middle school office to find out why my kid was doing so poorly in math. I would never have to ask the high school principal why the French teacher didn't seem to speak French. I would never have to ask the grade school principal why he rewrote my daughter's sixth-grade graduation speech to include more references to his prodigious sense of humor and caring disposition, and fewer jokes of her own.

I would never have to complain that the school had discontinued the Word Master's competition, the only activity at which my son excelled. I would never have to find out if my son was in any way responsible for a classmate breaking his wrist during recess. I would never again have to listen to my kid, or anyone else's kid, play the cello.

I would never have to attend a parent-teacher meeting to find out why my daughter's history professor was teaching that Edward II did not have a son. A son named Edward III. A son who took special pains to publicly hang the man who killed his dad—and let the body rot for a couple of days, just to show how ticked off he was about his father's mistreatment. All of which my kids knew because their mother grew up five miles from the castle where Edward II was heinously butchered. Leaving behind Edward III. His son.

"The time line gets confusing back then," the teacher explained when we visited him. No, it didn't. In history, this thing happened and that thing didn't. If you didn't know that, your students got crummy AP scores. And then they didn't get into the best college. My wife and I weren't going out of our way to embarrass the teacher. It was just . . . well . . . first you're wrong about Edward III, and then you're wrong about Henry III, and before you know it you're wrong about Richard III. Who knows where it all could lead?

But now it no longer mattered. The ordeal had ended; the eighteen-year plague had run its course; the bitter cup had passed from my lips. I would never quaff from its putrid contents again. Good riddance.

From the very beginning it was obvious that I was not going to enjoy my children's pedagogical experiences. Shortly after my daughter began nursery school, I was dragooned into serving as "Parent of the Day." There was nothing in my background or temperament to suggest that I was cut out for this kind of work. My daughter loved my serving in this capacity—in part because she knew that I would buy her pizza and ice cream after class—but I did not. Instead of slaving away in my office, something I loved doing, I had to spend two and a half hours listening to the teacher tell stories, serving the kiddies juice, taking the boys to the bathroom, and supervising the kids' playground activities. To this day, I have nightmares about Show and Tell. Long, horrible nightmares.

I can still recall sitting there, surrounded by annoying tots, gazing longingly at the clock, watching the second hand's torturous, interminable orbit, telling myself, "If I can just survive until it's time to wash the kids' hands, I might possibly get through this thing." The 150 minutes were excruciating. I felt every second dragging by. I once spent fifty minutes at the Spectrum in Philadelphia, listening to Jerry Garcia play a solo on "Truckin'." It was worse than that. I once spent two hours listening to John Tesh and a makeshift chamber orchestra at Carnegie Hall. It was worse than that. I once spent two hours watching five thousand pitiful ninnies reenact the Battle of Spotsylvania. It was worse than that. Being Parent of the Day was the most agonizing experience of my life, including the year I spent in Scranton. And I had to be Parent of the Day probably a dozen times over a four-year period.

To be a successful Parent of the Day, you had to really like children. I did not. I am not one of those parents who *only* like their own children, but I *am* one of those parents who only like their own children plus a couple of their closest friends. I lived in a prosperous suburban community, filled with young urban professionals, many of them lawyers or investment bankers, and a lot of the kids were at least as repellent as their parents. There were tons of entitled, self-involved, fiercely precocious little kids in that nursery school, and I didn't like any of them. I didn't like their clothes, I didn't like their attitudes, and I didn't like their names: Jared, Jackson, Jason, Jillian. There was something synthetic and twee about those kids. They made me sick.

As a freelance writer, I have labored mightily to avoid being in rooms with people I can't stand. This is why I have not had a day job since Dan Quayle was in office. But you can't avoid social congress with people you dislike when you're Parent of the Day. You're marooned, imprisoned, shackled. You're cast adrift in a lifeboat with a bunch of people you'd love to toss overboard. But can't. Because the people—and yes, children *are* people—are only four years old.

The teachers always found fault with my work as Parent of the Day. I gave some kids too much juice and some kids too little. I was insufficiently attentive to peanut allergies and self-esteem issues. I was no more than civil to the little kids I disliked, which violated the spirit of the nursery school experiment. When we finally went outside and I got to play the Big Bad Wolf or Dracula, I would terrify some of the smaller children and get the other ones all wound up, so they could not quiet down when they went back into class. The teachers found me distracting and annoying. I think I may have been the least successful Parent of the Day in the history of the school.

Years later, on a fifth-grade school trip to my hometown of Philadelphia, I jumped into the ornate fountain directly in front of the Franklin Institute. My daughter jumped in too. Her tie-dyed T-shirt dripped all the way home. The teachers on the trip were furious. They thought I was a jerk, an idiot, an insurgent, an irresponsible doofus. They had a point. Like I said, I was never cut out for this kind of stuff.

From nursery school on, everything involving my children's education was compensation for an earlier mistake. On the advice of a teacher, we gave our daughter "the gift of time" and had her repeat the last year of nursery school. (It occurred to me only later that this meant even more opportunities to be Parent of the Day.) The teacher said that our daughter was not socially mature. Or emotionally mature. Or something. Giving her the gift of time, she assured us, would mean that she would always be the oldest, and therefore the most confident, kid in class. As it turned out, it also meant that she would be the smartest kid in class. And because of this, she would spend her entire school experience without a proper peer group, mostly bored out of her mind.

The fallout from this decision never stopped reverberating. My daughter disliked her first kindergarten teacher so much that we had to get her transferred to another class. She thought some of her middle school and high school teachers were incompetent clowns. Some were. We had to arrange for her to jump from ninth-grade classes to tenth grade ones, because the work was so dull and her peer group was so weak. Then in twelfth grade she meandered back to eleventh, where the student body was much stronger than her own class, and there were many more AP courses for her to take. It was not a happy school experience.

On a happy note, she ended up going to Harvard. None of her peers from nursery school did. A lot of them were lucky to get into community college. Some might argue that holding her back a year and giving her the gift of time was what helped her get into Harvard. I disagree. We took stupid advice because we didn't know what we were doing at the time, and neither did the teacher. We were amateurs, which is a synonym for "parents." If we had not held our daughter back a year, she would have gone to Harvard twelve months earlier.

It is famously said that those who cannot remember the past are condemned to be Parent of the Day forever. And so it was with us. Oh yes, not content with the one foolish decision to hold our daughter back, we did the exact same thing with my son, making him repeat kindergarten, at the behest of the professionals. This was a humiliating experience that enraged him, because it permanently separated him from his peer group. For the next thirteen years, his best friends were always one year ahead of him. He never forgave us for this stupid move, nor can I think of any reason why he should. We thought we were making the right decision at the time, yes, but so did George Armstrong Custer. The results were similar.

My wife and I never regretted sending our kids to public school. We do not believe in private school; we believe that in a society such as ours, you are either on the bus or you are off the bus. The schools in our community were racially mixed, with about 50 percent minority representation, and a lot of parents pulled their kids out of the public schools when they got to sixth grade, rationalizing that they would not get a proper education otherwise. A lot of those kids ended up going to middling state schools or dumb-ass local colleges; my daughter went to Harvard, and my son got a free ride to law school. So the argument that public school would hold your kids back didn't exactly hold form for them.

That said, public school was no picnic for the kids. Public schools are designed to handle the vast majority of kids, but not special cases. They are not so good with kids at the top and not so good with kids at the bottom. A lot of my daughter's teachers got fed up with her bellyaching about the insipid materials and the languid pace of learning, and would have preferred that we pulled her out and sent her to some nauseatingly precious private school. That was not going to happen. Public school is the great litmus test of democracy; if you don't believe in public schools, you don't believe in America. (At least that's what we believe.)

That said, my daughter did not enjoy school. She recently

told me that the entire experience was a waste of time. She was insufficiently challenged and had no freedom. The whole thing was a twelve-year grind, for her as well as for us. I constantly had to explain to my daughter that most of her teachers were doing the best they could with the gifts they had. For some teachers, I noted, the profession was a civil service job, one step up from the post office. She had a few great teachers, and she had more than her fair share of duds. And she had a lot of teachers who resented kids like her who were clearly going places they had never been. A lot of teachers who were just scraping by. A lot of teachers who didn't have affluent parents. A lot of teachers who hadn't gone to Harvard. This kind of stuff is very hard to explain to a kid.

It was easier with my son, but only because he hated the very idea of school. Our daughter always wanted school to be more challenging and did not object to school per se; our son just wanted school to go away. He liked school even less after we pulled the kindergarten stunt. Yet in a way his uncompromisingly negative attitude made life easier. Unlike our daughter, who was always complaining about inept teachers and constantly trying to improve her educational environment, my son never complained that school was boring, that he hated his classes, that his teachers were dimwits, or that he needed work that was more intellectually stimulating. He just didn't like school. Full stop. He'd rather play sports or video games or stay at home watching movies and reading the books he wanted to read. He did not stop hating school until he went to college and got to major in classics.

My kids hated cant and they hated lies. They hated the bloodless, inanimate way history was taught to them. At dinner every night, they would pump me for the real truth about history, not the dreary, politically correct twaddle they were taught in school. They wanted to hear about the Holy Innocents, about Saint Lucy, about the Golden Horde, about the time a young

French archer fatally wounded Richard the Lionhearted, and on his deathbed Richard the Lionhearted said, "Don't do anything nasty to that feisty little kid," and his generals said "Okay." And then, about five minutes after King Richard died, they flayed the kid alive. They wanted to hear about Alexander the Great, Lady Godiva, Judas Iscariot, Erwin Rommel, Crazy Horse, the Spanish Inquisition, Vlad the Impaler, Marie Antoinette, the three hundred Spartans, the Maccabees, Masada, and unexpected nuances in Apache torture methods. They did not want to hear that the Iroquois lived in longhouses and respected women and had a governmental structure that exerted a profound influence on Thomas Jefferson. They wanted to hear about what the Iroquois did to their French Jesuit captives. They hated all that other crap.

There were other problems along the way. Personal problems. When my son was around fourteen he suddenly became very morose and angry. I asked him what was wrong, and he told me that a couple of kids at school were giving him a hard time. One kid had a particularly nasty turn of phrase. My son was a big kid; his tormenter was not. I asked him if he was afraid of the kid, and he said no. I told him to go to school the next day, grab the kid by the throat, jam him into an empty locker and say that he would knock all his teeth down his throat if he ever bothered him again.

"But I'll get suspended if I do that," he protested.

"Oh. I see. You'll get suspended and you'll have to spend a few days at home watching television. Where's the downside there?"

My son got a funny look on his face. He stopped being morose. He stopped being angry. He never told me what happened the next day at school. But I think that cheap punk got jammed right into a locker. My wife was mortified when she found out the advice I'd given my son. It seemed so crude, primeval. But it worked. As I explained to her at the time, we were both just doing the best we could with the resources available to us. We were making this stuff up as we went along.

Much of our experience as parents was figuring out ways to get our kids through the next school year. I told my son that I would buy him a new, powerful computer if he worked harder at French. His French grades got worse. We took the kids to Australia for two weeks one year in exchange for them no longer bellyaching about school. It was a long, brutal flight, but it meant no school for two weeks. They loved it. We took them to Los Angeles, Dublin, and Paris. They loved that, too. But we also took them to less glamorous places like Port Royal, Minneapolis, Aberdeen, Amiens, and Cardiff. They loved those places, too. One year we packed them up and took them to Raleigh-Durham for a week. They even enjoyed that. Weird kids. Anywhere I went for work, they were happy to go. Anything to get out of school. Anything.

We were not above resorting to bribes. The fact is, we could never have gotten my son through the last year of high school without (a) letting him drop soccer to play football, and (b) giving him my cobalt-blue 1983 Mercedes, which made him feel like a Teutonic god. Thank God (the real God) for loud, German, diesel-fueled cars. Truly, thank God.

There is a central paradox about being a parent and trying to get your kids to profit from their school experiences. You go into it as a parent hoping that your kids will be happy, all the while knowing that your own school experience was mostly miserable. You think you can make things better for your children, because surely things have changed since you were a kid—no more nuns with thick, fearsome rulers; no more priests who get a kick out of slapping young boys' faces—but in the end you can't save your kids from the inevitable. Because by and large school is an unpleasant experience. And you already know this because you went to school yourself.

The greatest American novel is *The Adventures of Huckleberry Finn*. It's about a kid who hates school. *Tom Sawyer* is about a kid who hates school. *The Catcher in the Rye* is about a kid who hates school, *A Separate Peace* is about a kid who hates school, and so are the *Harry Potter* books. School seems to be an almost universally unpleasant experience. You can try to sugarcoat it, yes, but you know from personal experience that school is horrid. There you are with all that imagination and all that energy and yet you're trapped inside all day reading books you don't want to be reading and learning things you don't want to be learning from teachers who mostly don't want to be teaching. Then one day it's all over and your kids leave and you find yourself staring at each other from either side of an empty nest.

And there's only one thing you can think to say to each other.

Thank God that's over.

CHAPTER 9

Sports

Advice for the Care and Feeding of the Child-Athlete

David Burge (aka Iowahawk)

THE JOYS OF FATHERHOOD are endless and nowhere more so than when it comes to the father-child bond of sports, hallucinated or otherwise. Walk into any hospital nursery ward, and you're sure to find row after row of sleeping newborns adorned in tiny NFL beanies and snuggling with cute little baseball gloves and footballs in their acrylic bassinets—gifts, no doubt, from proud fathers, eager to give their infants a head start on an enriching childhood full of active, healthy fun and vicarious paternal wish fulfillment. While these fathers certainly mean well, most have made a critical mistake: They waited until birth to begin molding their child for athletic stardom.

Studies show that by the time a child is three to four hours old, he may already be behind the curve on his/your plans for a career in professional sports. Just look at your neighbor, Mike Harberson, who was already down the hall in the neonatal room training his newborn to do bicycle kick exercises, while your wife wasted time coddling your son in her recovery room bed. If your son is going to have any chance at competing with the Justin Harbersons of the world, the key is early preparation.

Don't make the mistake of waiting until the last minute. By the third or fourth month of gestation, your wife is probably already playing Mozart for your womb-trapped athlete on the advice of her stupid Facebook friends. Here is your cue to add some Vince Lombardi speeches and the "Tomahawk Chop" chant to your athlete's uterine iPod mix. That way, by the time they cut his umbilical cord, he will have the psychological toughness necessary to remain focused for his winning drive at the 2035 National Championship game against Florida State, running to glory through the arm tackles of FSU girly-men raised on a prenatal musical diet of "Claire de Lune."

But if your (hormone-addled) pregnant wife insists on waiting until delivery to begin your child's athletic training, avoid bringing him the traditional birth gifts of fuzzy, soft miniature footballs and basketballs. Your newborn athlete deserves properly inflated, regulation-size equipment. Not only will this give him a head start on his maternity-ward peers, but they pose less of a choking hazard.

Before raising your child-athlete, it's critical to maintain realistic expectations. Many new dads harbor grand fantasies of their sons making millions in the NFL, NBA, or Major League Baseball. They have visions of sitting alongside him at draft day, throwing a proud fist in the air as Roger Goodell steps to the podium and announces his first-round selection, by the Dallas Cowboys, which causes a cascade of boos from disappointed Jets fans still enraged over the selection of Mike Harberson's stupid, overrated kid Justin with the previous pick. And then, after the big hat-fitting photo op with Jerry Jones—who, even in the year 2035, hasn't aged a day—the proud dad envisions his drive home in a brand-new, cash-filled, custom Escalade, given to him by his grateful, soon-to-be-Super-Bowl-MVP, millionaire son.

In reality, though, fewer than one out of three children will ever make it to the big leagues, according to some statistics I heard once on *SportsCenter*. While this may come as a shock, it doesn't mean sports can't still provide a lifetime of fulfillment to your child, as well as your retirement planning. For example, did you know baseball is extremely popular in Japan? It's true.

So even if your son gets passed over in the Major League draft, there's always the chance he could work his way up through the Nippon Ham Fighters organization. Similarly, there are professional basketball leagues in Greece and China, Mexican baseball, and Canadian football. So, as you raise your budding athlete, make sure to stock his training table with plenty of squid rolls, haggis, and poutine to prepare him for the rigors of life as a globe-hopping, mercenary jock-for-hire.

Of course, sports are not just a bonding experience between father and son. In the old days, some dads would find their vicarious dreams of gridiron fame crushed by the arrival of a baby girl. Luckily our society has moved beyond such outmoded thinking. Just because your daughter was cursed with two X chromosomes, it doesn't mean she needs to abandon her/your dream of international sports stardom. To the contrary—today's world provides many opportunities for the female athlete. For example, there is the WNBA, women's professional soccer, and the exceedingly popular Legends Football League, in which women play seven-on-seven tackle football. While wearing lingerie. This is also true.

A word of caution: While women's team sports continue to grow in popularity, the salaries pale in comparison to the men's big leagues. And many women's sports still have no professional associations. Tragically, your daughter-athlete could be stuck with nothing more than a four-year, full-ride, field hockey scholarship to Northwestern, with no professional career to pursue after graduation. But don't give up hope. Studies show that the *real* cash in women's sport is in individual competition, such as tennis, figure skating, and gymnastics, where big-time performers can earn as much as an NBA starter. Have I got your attention *now*, Mr. Sexist Neanderthal Dad? Yeah, I thought so.

Better yet, female athletes begin turning pro at a much younger age than their male counterparts, allowing you to retire to Hawaii on an accelerated schedule. Just look at the North Korean women's gymnastics squad, whose average age is approximately zygote. The key is to think ahead: Time your daughter's birth so that she will turn twelve in an Olympic year, then find a stern local Yugoslavian with a high-security lockdown figure skating camp. The camp's training bills and biannual visit policy will be hard at first. But before you know it you'll be eating Wheaties in Maui out of a box with your daughter's picture on it.

Even if you lucked out and had a son, it doesn't mean that you necessarily have to push him into the traditional "Big Three" of football, baseball, and basketball. If you can stomach the equipment and dental bills, there's always hockey. But don't let the fact that your son is not big enough or Dominican enough to participate in the he-boy sports keep him from potential stardom in other arenas. For example, soccer. Did you know that soccer is the most popular sport in the world, with billions of fans on every continent? Again, this is true. For whatever reason, there is a potential gold mine waiting in Europe for a scrawny, undersized kid if he can master the fine art of flopping to the grass while grabbing his knee.

But alternative sports don't stop at soccer. No matter his size or disposition, there is a sport waiting for your child to excel in it. Here are just a few of the possibilities:

- Wrestling: If your son can withstand the ceaseless conditioning, drills, and starvation diets required to be a competitive wrestler, he may eventually be rewarded with a scholarship to a midwestern state college and a face of lumpy cartilage.

- Track and field: The sport's biggest star, Usain Bolt, is also one of the richest, most recognized athletes in the world. Which is pretty great. Now try to name track and field's second-biggest star. You can't, because he works at a Starbucks between Olympiads. Also, your son is not Usain Bolt.
- Swimming and diving: See above; replace "Usain Bolt" with "Michael Phelps."
- Motor sports: The popularity of NASCAR and other racing leagues has spurred huge growth in youth motor sports. Success here requires quick reflexes, stamina, concentration, and a twelve-thousand-dollar toy that you will never be able to sell, even if he doesn't wreck it.
- Skateboarding: The explosive growth of skateboarding over the last twenty years means that there is probably a popular, nearby public skate park where your budding X-Games star can hone his skills. And by age thirteen, "Hey, Dad, I'm going to the skate park," will become code for, "Hey, Dad, I'm going to smoke some drugs."

On second thought, stick to football, baseball, basketball, and hockey. Or soccer, but only if it's absolutely unavoidable.

Now that your child has taken his first steps, it's time to assume your fatherly role as his first coach. Maintaining a healthy balance between a dad-son relationship and a coach-athlete relationship takes a combination of steady encouragement, patience, and positive reinforcement. Let's say you are in the backyard or at the park, instructing your toddler on the proper fielding stance, or how to place his fingers on the laces. During your coaching demonstration, your athlete is suddenly distracted by a nearby dandelion and wanders off. After retrieving him, walk him back to the field using fatherly encouragement to get him refocused on the task at hand. Then, after he is distracted by a grasshopper, encourage him to remove it from his mouth. When your repeated encouragements cause him to run sobbing to the consoling arms of your wife, who shoots you *that look* while mollycoddling him, wait patiently for a few minutes for the bawling to die down and your wife to give him a cookie. Voila! Your wife's positive reinforcement has now cemented in your athlete's mind a direct link between your coaching and free cookies.

As your child matures and his coordination improves to the point where it is no longer embarrassing, it will be time to turn him over to his first "non-dad" coaches. For most Americans, this occurs when you sign your child up for T-ball or youth soccer. In most cases, your child will now be in the hands of coaches who are fathers like you, dedicated to the proper development and fair treatment of your child-athlete. Or they could be biased, blind, passive-aggressive idiots, like Mike Harberson, who only volunteered to coach the team to make it a showcase for his stupid, glory-hogging kid, Justin.

To remedy such a situation, it may become necessary to volunteer as a coach yourself, if only to ensure that your child isn't overlooked should any college or pro scouts happen to drop by the park. A word of caution, though: This will require a serious commitment on your part, in terms of both time and money. Take a look at your aging, but serviceable, 2005 Honda Odyssey, for example. Do you really want to haul your son's team to postgame ice cream at Red Robin in that heap? Let's face it: Every kid on the team will be begging to go in the Harbersons' brand-new Suburban with its three DVD screens. Probably even your own kid. Come on, Coach—in the name of team unity, it's time to trade the minivan in for a Lincoln Navigator. Just remember: Like everything else in your life, you're doing this for *him.*

As your child begins competing on the field, among the most valuable lessons he will learn is sportsmanship. Postgame ceremonial high fives with his opponents will teach him the importance of being gracious in both victory and defeat. They also provide you the opportunity to teach him just how much easier it is to be a good sport after winning. And isn't honesty just as important a virtue to teach your child as sportsmanship? In my book, being frog-marched out to the middle of the field to mutter clearly insincere "good game" platitudes to a bunch of little dorks who just beat you hardly qualifies as "honesty." Thus, to maximize your child's chances of being an honest good sport, it is your sacred job as a father to make sure he never loses.

There are several ways you can help encourage your athlete's sportsmanship, even if the payments on your Navigator force you to stop co-coaching and take an extra job doing the night shift at Home Depot. First, when attending your child's games, emphasize the importance of fair play. Loudly and continually. Especially to the various Little League umpires and referees, who, in my experience, can be some of the most unfair idiots on planet Earth. If some loudmouth dad from the opposing team tries to interrupt you while you're correcting the umpire's bias, it may be necessary to further demonstrate your commitment to fair play with various hand gestures, or a well-aimed juice box to the head.

Even if your gallant efforts in the stands are not enough to prevent a humiliating loss, you can still emphasize good sportsmanship at the postgame team meeting. Remind everyone that they win together, and lose together, as a team. Make sure your child knows that you don't think any less of him for losing. Because it's not his fault he was stuck on a team with an incompetent skipper like Coach Harberson, who left Justin on the mound after giving up three straight hits and then sent Jake

Wilmot to bunt into a double play in the bottom of the eighth. When your son asks why you're not going to Red Robin, remind him that ice cream is for closers.

Middle school can be a harrowing time for the father of a growing athlete. By then he will be under the control of a stupid school coach who won't respond to your e-mails offering advice, no matter how many times you send them. It can also be harrowing for your athlete. Approaching puberty can bring about performance-limiting self-consciousness and self-doubt. It can also bring about uncontrollable boners. In your new role as his personal sports psychologist, use this fact of human biology to motivate your athlete for peak performance. For example, a few photos of Giselle Bündchen will help reinforce the importance of top quarterback technique. Studies show this is a more effective motivator than ice cream.

As your athlete enters high school, don't be overly concerned if he doesn't get immediate varsity playing time, even if he's obviously the best quarterback on the team. Sure, the coach would probably start him, except he can't bench a senior for a sophomore because of, you know, the politics. He's just keeping him in reserve on the JV team for next season. And he's probably keeping him on the JV bench to avoid injury.

Now it's your athlete's junior year in high school. This is it. The Show. Friday Night Lights. The high stakes, the big stage, complete with marching bands, cheerleaders, and concession stands. There will be actual paying crowds, probably teeming with scouts from Ohio State and Alabama who have secretly identified your son as a four-star prospect from last year's JV practice films. Unfortunately, after a titanic training camp battle, your son is robbed of his rightful starting job. When the coach remains deaf to your complaints, show support for your athlete by creating a "Bench Justin Harberson" Facebook page.

At the big season opener against West High—currently ranked eighth in the state's 4-AA Section II—you will be in the stands checking your phone to see how many likes your "Bench Justin" page has gotten. When West hits the field, you spy something, or rather someone, bursting from the tunnel: Holy crap, that kid is big. And I mean circus-freak HUGE, with speed to match. Haystacks Calhoun in shoulder pads, a full beard bushing out from his chinstrap. Then, for the first time in your life, you look over at a dumbstruck Mike Harberson with sympathy.

Midway through the second quarter, when a limping, mud-encrusted Justin Harberson is pulled from the field after another sack by the rampaging Haystacks Calhoun, you breathe a sigh of relief to discover your athlete is the *third*-string quarterback, behind the sophomore who now replaces Justin.

By the time your son gets in the game, it's 49-3. Mercifully, West has pulled its starters and you breathe another sigh of relief that he won't have to line up against Haystacks. You pump a proud fist when he scores his first high school touchdown, a garbage time bootleg with 1:36 left to go, but it's in a mostly deserted grandstand. After the game you walk down to the field to meet your son in the postgame handshakes and offer congratulations to West High's coach. "Man, your number 74 is one hell of a player," you'll say. "Who's recruiting him?"

"Oh, you mean Blake?" the coach will reply. "I think he has an offer to walk on at Indiana State."

It is at this point you will decide it may not hurt your athlete to miss a few practices to study for his AP chemistry test. When your son graduates, his yearbook photo will include in the caption "Football 1-2-3," and you will be completely fine with it.

Your son will go on to college, where, like you, his athletic career will consist primarily of in-dorm, pregame beer bongs. This will not help him achieve his/your dreams of pro sports stardom, but that's okay because he/you will no longer have those dreams. Plus sometimes he invites you to join in the beer bongs. Your new dream is that his/your old dream will gently fade, replaced by happy memories of the time you spent together—and that he will find a nice girl, settle down, and have a son of his own. And you already know he'll be a better athlete than Mike Harberson's grandson.

CHAPTER 10

The Dark Side

*Bad Parenting and the Things We Think,
but Do Not Say*

Toby Young

As a father of four children under twelve, I spend a lot of time trying to come up with better ways of getting them to do stuff that they don't want to do. And by "better" I don't mean more effective, because I've already discovered a method that works pretty well, which is to bribe them. Promising to let them play *Grand Theft Auto* next time their mum is out of the house usually does the trick, although cash works best. No, I mean a technique that their mother doesn't consider Exhibit A in the case for the prosecution against her deadbeat, useless husband.

A typical exchange between my wife, Caroline, and me goes like this:

> Caroline: Has Sasha done her homework?
> Me: What?
> Caroline: Her *homework*. She needs to do her homework before school on Monday.
> Me: She told me she didn't have any homework.
> Caroline: And you believed her I suppose?
> Me: You don't think she's lying, do you?
> Caroline: *Duh!*
> Me: Are you sure?
> Caroline: Have you checked her book bag?

Me: Her what?

Caroline: Her book bag. You know, *the bag she's been taking to school every day for the past seven years.*

Me: Yes, yes, of course.

Caroline: Well? Have you checked it?

Me: Where is it?

Caroline: The same place it always is.

Me: Where's that then?

Caroline: Where d'you think?

Me: If I knew I wouldn't ask.

Caroline: Oh, for God's sake.

Caroline is convinced that I am exaggerating my idiocy in order to make her life more difficult—that it's a form of "passive aggression," to use her phrase. But the truth is I *am* an idiot. Not in my day job, obviously. I've been earning a living as a freelance journalist for almost thirty years, and that's no small thing, particularly as journalists suffered an extinction-level event in 1991—the invention of the Internet. Thanks a lot, Al Gore.

But the fact that I've achieved a certain proficiency in my day job makes it that much harder to switch to my other job, which is being a father. It's as if, come 6:30 p.m., I'm forced to abandon the career I've devoted my life to and do a three-hour shift as an entry-level employee at a kindergarten. Actually, it's worse than that, because at the kindergarten I wouldn't be married to the person in charge. And even if I were, I would be entitled to various protections, such as not being asked whether I'm a "moron" when my boss discovers I'm using Krazy Glue to mend a piece of safety equipment—or, rather, a "*fucking* moron."

But I am a moron. Take the time Caroline put me in charge of buying Sasha some fish for her tenth birthday. It wasn't until we were in the pet shop that I discovered she had something more exotic in mind than goldfish. So I had to spend £100 on a fifty-liter tank, complete with a pump and an underwater heater. We were then faced with a dizzying array of tropical fish to choose from.

"How about some zebra fish?" said the sales assistant. "They fall into the category of 'hard-to-kill.'"

"Sounds good," I said.

We returned home with twelve zebra fish and began the process of introducing them to their new home. The most tedious part was standing beside my daughter as she painstakingly thought up names for them all.

By 6:00 p.m. I thought my labors were at an end, but no. Sasha came bursting into the kitchen in a state of hysteria, complaining that the pump wasn't working properly. I tramped back upstairs and discovered she was right. The pump was positioned behind a pane of black Plexiglas, creating a special chamber at the back of the tank, and for some reason it had managed to pump most of the water out of this chamber and was now making a continuous farting noise as it blew air into the rest of the tank. My solution was to push the filter deeper into the chamber until it was once again submerged.

"Are you sure that'll be alright, Daddy?" asked Sasha. "It's not going to hurt the fish?"

"They'll be alright. They're 'hard to kill,' remember?"

All was well until bedtime. At Sasha's insistence, I went with her to her room to check on the fish, only to find that they were not alright. The filter had emptied its chamber of the remaining water and was now sending a jet of air into the main tank with such force it had created a kind of fish Jacuzzi. Two of the fish had been propelled out of the tank and now lay dead on the carpet.

"Dad!" said Sasha. "You've killed Zip and Zap!"

I plunged my hand into the chamber to wrench out the pump, but somehow it had got wedged beneath the heater. So I removed that and placed it on the carpet next to Zip and Zap, at which point Sasha, who was hopping from foot to foot with anxiety, stepped on it.

"Aaaaaargh!"

Before I could tend to Sasha's foot, I still had to deal with the rogue pump, and in my haste I managed to break the pane of Plexiglas that separated the pump compartment from the rest of the tank. As the water levels equalized, the remaining ten zebra fish poured into the broken chamber and disappeared into the inner workings of the tank.

It was fishmageddon.

After Sasha had been sedated and removed from the room by Caroline, I set about repairing the tank. That involved emptying twenty-five liters of water so that I could stick the broken pane back together with Krazy Glue. By the time I'd completed the job and refilled the tank, I could only see two fish. They looked less like Zip and Zap than Float and Drift.

Anyway, as I was saying, I'm always trying to come up with ways of being a better dad, and one day I hit on a brilliant idea: I would use *The Prince* as a parenting guide. I took a class on Machiavelli in college, and it made perfect sense. He intended his book to be a practical guide to winning and holding on to power for would-be heads of state, but there is scarcely a field of human endeavor it hasn't been applied to, from seduction to the music business. Why not childcare? Nearly all disputes between parents and children are political at their root; they reflect the battle for mastery within the household. Who better to tell us how to prevail in these conflicts than history's most gifted political strategist?

For instance, I'd noticed that my bribery technique was losing some of its effectiveness, and Machiavelli explains why. In a chapter titled "Concerning Generosity and Frugality," he

points out that a prince who is overly generous will never succeed in winning over his subjects. They'll quickly start to think
that they're entitled to all that free stuff, and while they won't
give him any credit for keeping it coming, they'll resent him
if the gravy train grinds to a halt. Consequently, if he wants
to retain their loyalty, he has to spend more and more. "To
keep up his reputation for generosity, one will be obliged not to
neglect any form of ostentation," Machiavelli writes. "It follows
that a prince who so acts will inevitably dissipate all his wealth
in ostentatious displays." Conclusion: Better to be a tightwad.

Another example is chapter 11, in which Machiavelli praises
religion as a great tool of social control. Like many atheists,
I've often invoked a supernatural being to try and curb my children's bad behavior—step forward, Santa Claus. In the run-up
to Christmas, you only have to point out that Santa disapproves
of such-and-such a thing—getting down from the table before
you've finished your supper, for instance—to bring about
instant compliance. The thought that he might bring them a
lump of coal instead of the presents they've asked for is too
awful to contemplate.

The difficulty with this technique is that Santa doesn't have
God's all-seeing eye. As Sasha asked on one occasion, "How will
he *know* if I don't eat my broccoli?"

I had to be careful how I answered this. I didn't want to
say that I would tell him myself, since that would conflict with
another lesson I had been trying to teach her, namely, that it is
wrong to tattle.

Then, inspired by Machiavelli, I had a brainwave. "You see
that little gizmo," I said, pointing to the motion detector in the
corner of the room that was connected to the burglar alarm.

"Yes," she said.

"That's Santa's CCTV. He's got this big bank of screens in
the North Pole, and there are these elves that sit there, day and
night, monitoring every child's behavior. Whenever the little
red light comes on, that means they're watching you."

She looked up, eyes wide with astonishment, then immediately started eating her greens. Bingo! Emboldened by this success, I drew up a list of Ten Commandments and pinned them to the fridge:

1. No child will be permitted to leave his or her room until 7:00 a.m. If anyone wakes up before this, he or she will have to amuse themselves <u>in their room</u> until it is time to come downstairs, at which point they will appear fully dressed and ready for school. Under no circumstances will any child wake up Daddy and ask him to get them dressed.

2. Breakfast will consist of a glass of water and hot porridge. No juice and DEFINITELY no Cheerios.

3. After breakfast, teeth will be cleaned uncomplainingly. Teeth must be brushed for <u>at least</u> three minutes. Daddy is permitted to use a stopwatch to ensure compliance.

4. Any time between finishing breakfast and going to school will be spent doing homework or practicing a musical instrument. No screens!

5. On the school run, all children will sit quietly in their assigned seats, with seatbelts tightly fastened. No fighting and no games of tag! Daddy will choose the radio station, and if he chooses to listen to the news, no one is allowed to protest by shouting "blah, blah, blah" at the top of their voice.

6. Children returning from school will not be cranky. Demands for a "snack" will be met with a piece of fresh fruit.

7. All "artwork" will be examined, praised, and then placed in a drawer, never to be looked at again.

8. Supper will consist of organic vegetables, a healthy cereal like quinoa or freekeh, and a piece of lean protein, e.g., fish. Sausages will only be served once

a week, and potato chips cannot be substituted for vegetables.

9. Daddy will read all children a bedtime story. They are only allowed to choose one story each. All objections to other people's choice of story will be ignored.

10. All children will be in bed with their lights out by 8:30 p.m. Appearing in Mummy and Daddy's room in the middle of the night and claiming to be "scared" is strictly <u>verboten</u>. Under no circumstances will Daddy swap places with any child so they can sleep with Mummy.

Reading this back now, I laugh at my naïveté. *No Cheerios?!?* Pah! In order to apply *The Prince* to any area of life, you need certain manly qualities, what Machiavelli called "virtù," and I simply don't have them. I used to, back in my youth. But I handed them over to Caroline when we got married, and she has kept them in her purse ever since.

Okay, I'm exaggerating slightly. I'm not a completely surrendered husband. I'm torn between accepting my place at the bottom of the household hierarchy and challenging the status quo. As recently as fifty years ago, guys like me still lived in a *Mad Men* universe, but the sexual revolution put paid to that; and it's not clear what the point of us is, other than to open pickle jars. What Dean Acheson said of postwar Britain is also true of modern fathers: We have lost an empire and have yet to find a role.

Until recently, I used to worry about the impact this would have on my children. According to Dr. Freud, children only develop a moral compass if they are told very firmly by their fathers what they can and can't do. It is the voice of the father, reprimanding them for behaving badly, that becomes internalized in the form of the "superego," or conscience.

I'm not such a dinosaur that I think mothers are incapable of playing this role, and I'm sure many of them do. But whose voice becomes internalized in households where authority is diffused and contested? One of the consequences of the women's rights movement is that many of the more affluent homes in the developed world lack an authority figure. Patriarchy has been swept away, but it hasn't been replaced by matriarchy, at least not yet. It's something closer to *kindergarchy*, a word coined by the late humorist Sam Levenson to describe a state of affairs in which children rule the roost. That can't be good for them, surely? They'll grow up to be spoiled brats with a gargantuan sense of entitlement.

As I say, I used to be concerned about this, but then I read a book by Judith Rich Harris called *The Nurture Assumption*. This book, which has been hailed as a milestone in the field of child psychology, is based on an article Harris wrote for an academic journal called *Psychological Review*. It began with these words: "Do parents have any important long-term effects on the development of their child's personality? This article examines the evidence and concludes that the answer is no."

I won't rehash Harris's argument in detail, but it's highly persuasive. After examining numerous studies of twins separated at birth, as well as adoptive siblings who grew up in the same family but have different biological parents, Harris concludes that nature is a lot more important than nurture. Most of our personality traits are embedded in our DNA. Insofar as a child's environment does have an impact on personality, the key factor is the child's peer group, not her parents. Contrary to the assumptions made by Freud and the psychologists who followed in his wake, Mum and Dad have practically zero effect on how their kids turn out.

If you're an anxious father, I highly recommend Harris's

book. It's like a Homer Simpson Manifesto. If your kids end up unemployed, or working as strippers, or even as unemployed strippers, they can't blame you. Because of it, I've stopped worrying about my hopeless parenting and now spend my time trying to persuade my children to hang out with the class nerds. That's pretty much all you can do: Give them a roof over their heads, load them up on Cheerios, and hope they pick good friends.

Fathers of the world unite. It doesn't matter how crappy you are, your kids will probably turn out okay. You might as well settle into a comfy chair, open another beer, and switch on the TV.

CHAPTER 11

The Talk

*The Birds and Bees Aren't What They
Used to Be*

Matt Labash

IT IS DIFFICULT for any man to be an impartial observer of
his own life, so far be it from me to grade my own facility in
the sack. It seems presumptuous to award bonus points for all
the ecstatic moaning, rapturous wailing, and "oh-yes!" incan-
tations, since technically speaking, another lover isn't always
present. (As the ethicist Stephen Stills says, "If you can't be
with the one you love, love the one you're with.") But when I
do log some business-time with my lady friend, if I do anything
at all laudable, I can say with earnest humility that it is not me
to whom she should offer thanks, but rather to my twin sex-
education senseis—*The Waltons* and Dr. James Dobson.

To rewind a little, I don't mean to paint my younger self
as a rube. But in the cloistered, early '80s, South Texas Bible-
belt environment in which I spent a healthy chunk of youth, I
lacked a certain sophistication that only came to me later, after
watching lots of Cinemax. For instance, after scandalous word
spread that a seventh-grade Sunday school classmate—a hot
little number who tottered around on unsteady wedges and
lacquered her lips in a shade of pink the color of watermelon
Bubblicious—was bounced from her parochial school for giving a boy a blowjob on the bus, I thought, *That's odd, why would
they expel her for blowing someone a kiss? Seems pretty harmless to me.*

Though I, too, struggled with my own dark stirrings of the flesh, PG edition. I was inflamed with lust over the Dallas Cowboys cheerleaders and two-thirds of *Charlie's Angels*. (Farrah and Jaclyn Smith—only later, when Kate Jackson achieved full flower during her *Scarecrow and Mrs. King* phase, did I realize it should've been three-thirds. With age comes wisdom.) I'd also entertain lascivious thoughts when spying the humid, inviting calves of one of the "wilder" girls in our buttoned-up Christian school, as she'd hike her P.E. culottes a quarter inch above the knee, in flagrant violation of our strict dress code and/or God's law. We were never clear on where, precisely, the Good Book regulated hem lengths, but were reassured by those in the know that it had to be in there somewhere. (When in doubt, check Leviticus.)

And while our parents tried to limit our listening habits to Amy Grant, Petra, and other insufferable contemporary Christian rock offerings of the day, we'd frequently sneak the secular hard stuff. One of those summers' sex-drenched musical staples was the Steve Miller Band's "Abracadabra." As we crowded around our friend Kenny's ghetto blaster, we might as well have been shooting black-tar heroin while singing along:

> I feel the magic in your caress
> I feel magic when I touch your dress
> Silk and satin, leather and lace
> Black panties with an angel's face.

In the fullness of time, I realize how ridiculous that sounds. "I feel magic when I touch your dress"? Did the Gangster of Love write this song in the shower five minutes before leaving for the studio to record it? And silk, satin, leather, *and* lace? I'm no fashion authority. But how many fabrics can one dress contain before it's no longer "magic," but a Blackwellian traffic snarl—something Björk might wear to the Icelandic Music

Awards, or Stevie Nicks to a Wicca convention? Still, Miller spoke to me, and continues to speak to me, if I'm being honest, with "black panties with an angel's face." He was signaling an adult world of erotic mystery, of which I then had only the slightest intimation.

I sang along knowingly but didn't know nearly as much as I pretended. That's when my sexual awakening occurred, thanks to a *Waltons* rerun. I watched the show religiously in those days, and not just because I wanted Mary Ellen Walton to be my older sister so I could watch her bathe through the bathroom keyhole. There was a specific episode—the details escape me now—in which one or another Walton sibling got someone in the family way. With approximately ninety-seven people in that family, someone tended to always be in the family way on Walton's Mountain. They were a poor, but fertile people.

This plot twist left me confused, though. The Walton boy and his girlfriend weren't even married. I thought married people had babies. But despite my Talmudic studies of Mr. Miller's "Abracadabra," I still wasn't 100 percent certain on the grim particulars of how a baby was actually produced. This warranted further parental inquiry. "Just to be clear, Mom," I said, a persistently curious child for one of such average intelligence, "did the Walton boy get his girlfriend pregnant because they slept in the same bed?" My mother looked a bit crestfallen, as though she'd hoped I'd already picked up this information where all Southern Baptist kids whose repressive religious school doesn't have sex-education classes tended to—on the street, or while watching *Porky's II* over at Steven Todd's house. (He had cable.)

So she did what any good Christian woman of that time and place did—passed the buck to my dad. "It's time for you and your father to have a talk," she said.

My military-officer father was a loquacious type, unafraid to hold us hostage for hours at the dinner table. One night he might choose to expound on the proper topsoil-to-fertilizer ratio for ideal carpetgrass. Or perhaps he'd further our moral instruction by reading from a multivolume set of *Character Sketches*, in which biblical truths were fleshed out with wildlife stories, so that my sister and I might emulate the determination of the cecropia moth or the orderliness of the woodchuck.

Yet when it came to The Talk, he fell strangely mute. I waited for days, trying to piece together the mystery of *The Waltons* on my own. In those pre-Internet times, the dumb stayed dumb a lot longer. Finally, late one afternoon, I heard the click-clack of his perma-shined Corfam uniform shoes marching toward my room. Filling the doorway, he tossed me a paperback. "I understand you had some questions for your mom," he said. "Read this, and tell me if you have any others."

And that was it. Confused by this laconic, Gary Cooperesque figure in my room, I watched my dad take off like he'd received an evacuation order. He left my room so quickly, I thought maybe it was my pits. (It was high puberty, and my body was changing.) But I dug into his little instruction manual—*Preparing for Adolescence*, written by leading Evangelical light Dr. James Dobson—like a Sudanese war orphan digging into a U.N. corn meal provision.

I skimmed all the boring stuff about the "secrets of self-esteem" and every adolescent's trip through the "canyon of inferiority." The money chapter was titled "Something Crazy Is Happening to My Body," and there on page 60—which I practically committed to memory—Dr. Dobson laid it out matter-of-factly. He explained how sexual intercourse "is the name given to the act that takes place when a man and woman remove their clothing (usually done in bed)." Then he detailed what happens to the man parts and where they go vis-à-vis the woman parts. If you've had sex, you know. If you haven't, that's why

God invented Google—so that we don't have to have this sort of awkward conversation.

Anyway, Dobson went on: "They move around, in and out, until they both have a kind of tingly feeling which lasts for a minute or two," concluding that this act is "something that makes a husband and wife very special to each other." Laugh if you will at Dr. Dobson's churchy carnality. But considering the average male orgasm lasts eight seconds, and the average female's about twenty, Dr. and Mrs. Dobson must have been onto something with their tingly feelings. A minute or two?

Abracadabra, indeed.

In keeping with longstanding filial tradition, the next time my father and I even obliquely discussed sex was when I was handing him his grandkids some two decades later. When I asked him recently at a family dinner if he learned about sex from having The Talk with his dad, his nostrils nearly turned into iced-tea sprinklers. "No!" he laughed, trying to recompose himself, "I learned about it when I was eight—on the street. Where'd ya think?"

It's a general truism that most fathers regard giving The Talk as an activity on a par with getting a prostate exam from a doctor with Marfan syndrome, marrying their daughter off to a Boko Haram child soldier, or sitting through an entire episode of *The View*. It's a horror to be avoided at all costs.

Professional sexperts, of course, such as one at healthychil -dren.org, like to remind us that "if you don't educate them, someone else will." Well, yes. Historically, that's kind of what we were hoping for. We outsource every other unpleasant task in this country. What makes The Talk think it's so special? As long as immigrants are flooding over the border to pick our lettuce and tack up our siding, why don't they do something truly useful? My kids are required to take Spanish in school. I'd have been perfectly happy to turn them over to Pedro the Yard Guy, so he could explain to them *dónde vienen los niños.*

But leaving our children to "the street," particularly now that the street has gone virtual, isn't what it used to be. If the fabled street used to resemble some otherwise sunny thoroughfare in a shade-tree suburb, where a freckled ruffian in a newsboy cap called *pssst* from behind the egg-cream shop, asking if you want to see his dad's skin mag for a quarter, it now resembles something closer to a child prostitution ring on the east side of Detroit. It's not a place you'd want to go to unless you're a first responder or a German tourist.

As a friend with four tech-savvy children (which is to say all children these days) once warned me, "Before you ever give The Talk, be aware that your kids have probably seen at least a hundred hours of the vilest, most unspeakable pornography you can possibly imagine." Well, maybe. But when my wife did a search history inspection of a communal house computer recently, the saltiest search she found was for "Selena Gomez and panties." And that very well could have been mine. After all those hours of dutifully watching Disney Channel's *Wizards of Waverly Place* with my kids like some sort of henpecked, proactive father, a man's mind can turn to wanderin'.

But the sexperts are right. There is much incentive to take The Talk into your own hands these days so that your kids don't learn about sex from Internet porn. Or from the underemployed basketball coach who's avoiding layoff by teaching the sex-ed class in their school—where he's probably telling your children that the most important thing about sex is to stay on their parents' insurance so that they're covered if they have to get shots for the clap.

Or you may be interested in avoiding the most insidious influence of all: the well-meaning, overexplaining sexperts themselves. I've just read a tall stack of their scribblings, and I might be more comfortable entrusting my kids to the educators from YouPorn.com.

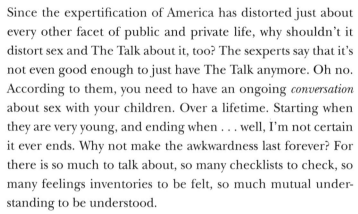

Since the expertification of America has distorted just about every other facet of public and private life, why shouldn't it distort sex and The Talk about it, too? The sexperts say that it's not even good enough to just have The Talk anymore. Oh no. According to them, you need to have an ongoing *conversation* about sex with your children. Over a lifetime. Starting when they are very young, and ending when . . . well, I'm not certain it ever ends. Why not make the awkwardness last forever? For there is so much to talk about, so many checklists to check, so many feelings inventories to be felt, so much mutual understanding to be understood.

In the digital masturbatorium that America has become, Dr. Ruth Westheimer, in *Dr. Ruth's Guide to Teens & Sex Today*, instructs parents that we might need to consider giving our children "replacement porn and erotica"—perhaps a copy of *Lady Chatterley's Lover*, or a comparatively tasteful *Playboy* subscription, so that they don't go looking for the hard stuff at analjunglegym.edu. Slide them Anaïs Nin's *Delta of Venus*, and you "might help them to masturbate, but you'll also be exposing them to good literature," writes America's favorite sex gnome.

Or you could take Amber Madison's advice from *Talking Sex with Your Kids,* even though she was only twenty-five when writing it and didn't technically have any kids. Still, she wants to stand as a generational go-between, to make sure "teens' voices are accounted for." "Do you really want your child's sexual health information coming from the phys ed teacher with the tacky wind pants, bad attitude, and IQ just high enough to explain the rules of dodgeball?" Amber asks. Of course not. You want it to come from Amber, who, coincidentally, wrote another book called *Hooking Up: A Girl's All-Out Guide to Sex and Sexuality*, and whose parenting expertise comes from studying human sexuality at Tufts.

Amber instructs us to say "penis," "vagina," and "sex" out loud, and over and over again, to desensitize ourselves to the embarrassment of talking to our kids about sex. After that, we need to do the same with "oral sex," "anal sex," and "vaginal lubrication" as well. (Picturing my own dad, standing in a corner, psyching himself up for The Talk with a "vaginal lubrication" chant—I'd much rather have been put up for adoption or gone with the phys ed teacher in the tacky wind pants.)

Then there's the widely-heralded gay sex educator Al Vernacchio, who, when not being featured in the *New York Times Magazine*, teaches sexuality at a private Quaker high school in Pennsylvania. Perhaps you've seen his TED talk (1.3 million views) where his deep insight (later fleshed out in his book, *For Goodness Sex*) is that sex needs a new metaphor to replace baseball.

For too long, Vernacchio argues, baseball has served as a cretin's shorthand for sex, what with all its talk of bases and "scoring" and whatnot. After all, in our hyper-sexualized society, who can even agree what the bases are anymore? Is vanilla intercourse even still considered a home run? Or are you now hitting a home run just by not drowning in a puddle of bodily fluids at the bottom of a naked dogpile? (Tom Wolfe once suggested that in a hookup culture that's so successfully decoupled intimacy from sex, third base now meant "going all the way, and 'home plate' meant learning each others' names.")

Vernacchio, for his part—as befitting someone who is faculty moderator of his school's Gay-Straight Alliance and who believes it is "disrespectful and imprecise" to use limited words like "male" and "female" to "explore a diverse reality"—thinks baseball/sex metaphors are a crime against humanity.

"Sex as baseball isn't just sexist," Vernacchio writes. "It's homophobic, it's competitive. It's goal-directed, and it's unlikely to result in the healthy development of sexuality in young people." So what's the answer? A soccer substitute? The kids all play soccer. But what on earth is a "banana kick" supposed to be in relation to sex?

No, Vernacchio says "pizza" is the correct metaphor. Pizza connotes "positive associations." It's a noncompetitive "shared experience" that's "satisfying for both of us." His pizza model, he says, isn't about inflicting will, but asking questions to foster mutual enjoyment:

"What do you like on your pizza?"

"How many slices do you want?"

"If I eat your anchovies, will you eat my sausage?"

Confession: That last question was mine. That was me trying to be the bad boy—though like Vernacchio, I prefer gender-neutral terminology and reject binary heteronormative distinctions as I am constantly evolving on a journey of self-discovery. (The bad person?) But Vernacchio is serious.

Though not as serious as Dr. John T. Chirban, in his *How to Talk to Your Kids about Sex*—which is not to be confused with Linda and Richard Eyre's *How to Talk to Your Child about Sex.* Neither of which are to be confused with Dr. Laura Berman's *Talking to Your Kids about Sex,* in which Dr. Berman asks the question every parent should answer themselves before attempting to instill a "healthy genital self-image" in his or her child: "Do you think it is important to feel good about your genitals?"

However you feel about your genitals, perhaps you thought conveying simple information about the propagation of the species—which, after all, has been going strong for millennia without sexpert oversight—was a relatively straightforward affair. (My twelve-year-old son, whom I wanted to make sure retained the information a few years after his own Talk, recapped it as such: "Yeah, Dad—the hot dog goes in the bagel." Not as elegant a formulation as I'd hoped for, but it was nice to see that the raw essentials took.)

Dr. Chirban isn't quite as loosey-goosey: He amps reluctant

parents up for The Talk by giving them a battery of preparatory tests. On page 21, there's the Strengthening Your Bonds and Connections questionnaire. On page 38, there's the Sexual Wholeness flowchart. On page 41, there's the General Information Quiz on Sexuality. On page 46, there's your Sexual Values position grid. On page 76, there's the Balance of Attunement Core Qualities chart. (The perfect balance between "being permissive" and "judging" is "accepting.") On and on it goes.

By the time you fill out all of Dr. Chirban's exercises, you may be having The Talk with your grandchildren, not your children.

I mock the sexperts because they've earned it. But in fairness, they're just trying to wrap their heads around The Talk, that troubling, peculiar beast. With other knowledge we impart to our children—whether it's how to throw a perfect spiral, or ride a bike, or catch a fish—we expect them to employ their newly-learned skills immediately. Yet when it comes to telling them about sex, we hope, and even pray, that they don't. That they sit on and defer the knowledge that will effectively end their childhoods. Children, being the only thing we've ever known them to be.

It can feel as though we're still preserving yesterday's fictions while revealing tomorrow's truths, which makes for an uncomfortable tension. But who ever said that fatherhood was going to be comfortable? As an older friend informed me after my first son was born in my twenties: "Just remember that we don't make adults of our children. They make adults out of us."

And so it went in my own Talk with my firstborn son, Luke. He'd gone a little past due in subscribing to Santa. My wife, Alana, and I worried that he might become the object of fifth-grade sport if we didn't soon shatter his illusions. When I broke the news to my guileless progeny, he didn't believe me. Instead, he checked with his mom to make sure I wasn't lying.

A few weeks later, Alana broke some news of her own. It was time, she'd decided, that Luke was given The Talk. "I wish you well," I told her sincerely. "Not me," she said, "it's time for *you* to give him The Talk." I was sickened by her cowardice.

"You mean about the Tooth Fairy?" I played dumb.

"No," she replied curtly. "That jig was up long ago. *The* Talk. The Sex Talk."

Here I'd just spoiled the little sucker's Christmases for the rest of his days, and now his own mother was asking me to reorder his world all over again. Theoretically, I suppose, it was a good-news/bad-news proposition. Yes, Santa wouldn't be visiting any longer. But with the new information I was about to impart regarding God's beautiful gift of physical union, in time, it could be Christmas every day—in his pants.

It's not that I'd never broached any sexual topics with the kids. They didn't think babies came from Home Depot. Or at least I'm pretty sure they didn't. I'd straightforwardly instructed them that male privates are called "chickens," while female privates are called "wookies." I'd told them that there was "good touch" and "bad touch," and that if a sweaty man in a work van ever offered them a lift, it was likely to be a bad-touch situation. I'd covered the basics.

But somehow, this new Christmas bait-n-switch didn't feel like I was bearing Luke good tidings of great joy. It felt like something was ending that he wasn't yet ready to be over. Or maybe I wasn't. We loaded up our tandem kayak—him sitting in the bow, me in the stern, staring at the back of his head. I was there to tell him how to be a man, but the last thing I wanted to do was look him in the eye like one.

We paddled down the slow, muddy, southern Maryland river through the marshes where I'd taken him since before he could talk, every bend reminding me of something a younger him had said or done. There was the spot where he once asked, "Does God have knees?" The place where he once bellowed his favorite Christmas carol, "Mark and Harold Angel Sing."

There was the run where he asked, "Daddy, are testicles just for decoration?" And the bank where I'd let him relieve himself, after his bladder had been taxed from too many Capri Suns. I had steadied the boat by grabbing a blade-full of river bottom, as Luke stood up, dropped trou, and squirted the spatterdock like a fountain cherub in a Florentine piazza.

As we spied the box turtles and beavers, the red-winged blackbirds and the blue herons, I envied our wildlife brethren for not having to have the conversation with their spawn that I had to have with mine. But I finally plunged in anyway, telling Luke about the whole M&M cycle—from menstruation to masturbation, and all points in between. In my own language, I filled him in on the Dobsonian particulars, minus the two-minute tingles. (Why put undue pressure on the kid?)

The rest of what I told him is mostly a blur, except when my fear dissipated and my male vanity kicked in. If I was going to tell my son how to have sex, I might as well tell him what I wish someone had told me—how to be good at it. "Luke," I confided conspiratorially, "there's this very little, very special spot on a woman, that when the time is right, and you've found your soul mate, you should pay really close attention to. Professional anatomists call it 'the little man in the boat.'"

It went on like that for a good while, until I finally punched myself out. "Do you have any questions?" I asked my son. He had only two.

"Can we be done?" he implored. "You know I think this is gross, right?"

By any objective sexpert's standard, my Talk had failed miserably. Or had it? I wasn't sure. I'd probably scared my son off of sex for a good while by overloading him with too much detail. But maybe scaring him wasn't the worst thing. The modern assumption is that laying mysteries bare is always better. Sharing is caring. But a little healthy fear and ignorance can be just as useful. That which intimidates us can keep us from barreling headlong into a mistake. As someone with no mechanical expertise, for example, I'm much less likely to try to change the timing belt in my car, possibly screwing up my engine forever.

Similarly, sex is strange and wondrous, a beautiful thing. When it hits on all cylinders, it's perhaps the most beautiful thing. But children shouldn't be having it, because sex also carries a weight they are not yet equipped to bear. It's too easy to make grievous mistakes when you're still a kid. Hell, it's not all that difficult when you're an adult. (Consider that, if current figures hold, you have almost a 50 percent chance of being divorced and a 40 percent chance of having had a child out of wedlock.)

Talk shows and tabloids are loaded with stories about our promiscuous youth, with everything from "sex bracelets" to "blowjob parties." While these are largely the stuff of urban legend and desperate trend spotters, it's not a stretch to believe that our children are looser than children once were. After all, look who they have for parents and grandparents. And yet, the average age of first intercourse is still right around seventeen, which is actually higher than it was two decades ago. It's probably true that our children aren't always as innocent as we'd hope. But neither should we assume that they're as guilty as we fear.

If sex intimidates our kids a little, maybe it should. We should all have a healthy awe of something that can alter our lives in every imaginable way. If I were giving The Talk all over again, I would tell my son that even if his body is ready, his soul and spirit aren't. And without those three things being of one accord, having sex is like eating your favorite chili without a spoon. It might taste good, but you're gonna burn your fingers and make an awful mess besides.

Of course, I should've had another crack at The Talk, since I have a younger son. But Dean is not as naïve as his older brother. When we tried to keep the Santa ruse going with him, he spied discarded boxes in the garage, asking us accusatorily, "If Santa makes our toys, why do they come in boxes with store barcodes?"

Nor does he seem as reflexively innocent. One of his favorite stunts is to exit the shower buck naked, come downstairs, open the pantry door, and grab a snack. As the family looks on in gape-mouthed horror, Dean will say, "Whoa! What are you looking at? My eyes are up here."

But when it came time for his Talk, my wife decided she'd take matters into her own hands. Considering my prior failure, I didn't fight her. Misery loves company. And if she missed any fine points—like the little man in the boat—I could always fill him in later.

As Alana set about descending on Dean, his older brother, still scarred from our Talk, tried to intervene. "What are you telling him?!!!" Luke protested. But Dean was ready. Even if he didn't know exactly what was coming, he sort of did, perhaps inherently mindful of the Teacher's admonition in Ecclesiastes: "He who increases knowledge increases sorrow."

As he pushed up his sleeves, hiked himself up on the counter, and awaited my wife's bombshell, he announced, "Alright, innocence ending. Childhood is over."

Don't rush it, little man. That's the kind of talk your pop's not ready to hear just yet.

CHAPTER 12

Dating

*Enjoy the Movie and Please Keep the
Impregnation to a Minimum*

Michael Graham

HERE'S THE FIRST THING you need to know about dads and dating:

When you say "date," we think "sex."

When you say "boy," we think "sex."

When you say "go out," or "see a movie," or "he's just a friend," we think "sex," "sex," and "club him into a coma with a tire iron."

That's because we're dads.

However, we also think "sex" when we hear other words. Words like "apple pie." Or "tea cup." Or "exhaust manifold." Or "spatula"—definitely "spatula." In fact, we think "sex" with pretty much *any* random word snatched from the Scrabble dictionary. And that's because we're *guys*.

Remember in high school English class when your teacher talked about the categories of existential conflict? Man versus nature. Man versus man. Man versus himself. Well, those are petty squabbles compared to the epic struggle unleashed when a father finds out his daughter is heading out on her first date, when it becomes Dad versus Guy.

The dad part of our brain screams, "Touch my daughter, and I'll kill you." But the guy part of our brain is whispering, "Dude, that's kind of awesome." When we see a teenage boy knock on the door across the street, our primeval, Cro-Magnon brain sends out a high five. But if that same boy realizes he's at the wrong house, crosses the street, and knocks on *our* door, we start contemplating the finer points of chemical castration.

How can we hate them when we *were* them? How can we declare that our little girl's not dating until she gets her AARP card, when our entire youth was little more than the dogged pursuit of other dads' daughters? When our own high school years were basically a series of humiliating incidents of social failure and extreme embarrassment, concluding with a half-baked explanation about why we were under the bleachers with a Polaroid during cheerleading practice. (Or maybe that was just me.)

Yet here we are. Through a combination of divine intervention and sympathetic bartending, even *I* somehow managed to marry and reproduce. I'm now the proud father of two precious daughters, one who recently started college and one who will soon be in middle school.

I also have two sons, but when the topic is dads and dating, honestly, who cares about them? Has any father lost sleep over his son's dating decisions? The eventual prospects of marriage and fatherhood make us worry about the boys. The idea that they might hack into our laptop and find NaughtyNurses.net in the browser history—that's how they keep us up at night. But them dating? As my daughters say, whatevs. Feminists fighting the heteronormative oppression of patriarchal hegemony can complain all they want, but fathers just don't carry around the same anxiety about their sons. My own dad was perfect example.

My Evangelical father was an involved parent who spent hours teaching me everything from biblical eschatology to routine auto maintenance. We worked in his TV repair shop together, he quizzed me on trivia, we even spent a weekend on a "family time" retreat playing "the UNgame"—a board game marketed as a fun way to promote interfamily communication. (It resembled "fun" in the same way that waterboarding resembles a log flume.) By any measure, my dad took parenting pretty seriously.

But when it came time to have The Talk, his entire dating advice to me consisted—literally—of a single sentence: "Michael," he declared gravely one Sunday morning as he drove us to church, "your mother says I need to talk to you about girls. So I'm gonna say my piece right here where she can hear it."

"Simon, please . . . ," my mother squeaked, but Dad had his game face on.

"Son . . ." There was a pregnant pause. "Keep your pants zipped until you're married." He shifted the Datsun into fifth gear, cranked up the gospel music on the cassette deck, and we never spoke of it again.

To be sure, things have changed in the intervening years, but not much. Research shows that contemporary dads are somewhat more involved in conversations about dating and relationships and, ahem, "spatulas." But even so, what we tell our sons is very different from what we tell our daughters. A recent study published in *Evolutionary Behavioral Sciences* found that while similar percentages of college-age sons and daughters reported talking about sex with parents in their early teens, daughters were more likely to get messages regarding abstinence, self-control, curfews, and the like.

The one message parents gave to boys more often than girls? "Have fun." Now that's "guy" talk.

But daughters? Our precious, innocent, starry-eyed princesses who can get us to max out our Amex with a single smile? What should we do about them when boys begin prowling around? I know what you're thinking. You think you're going to be a hard-liner: *I'm going to have rules, Michael*—Rules! *No dating until she's thirty! A five o'clock curfew, and none of that pulling-into-the-driveway-and-honking crap, either. You honk in my driveway, then you better be dropping something off, because you ain't pickin' anyone up.* I've talked to plenty of guys with young daughters who've already prepared a first-date scenario: The nervous boy sits on the living room sofa tugging uncomfortably at his collar while Dad cleans a shotgun and mutters disturbing phrases about PTSD and anger-management class.

Here's the problem, Daddy Dead-Eye. Kids don't actually (to paraphrase Whoopi Goldberg) "*date* date" anymore. Today, teenage boys rarely do the "Hi, Mr. Melman, I'm here to pick up Angela" bit. I discovered this from my own teenage daughter. Instead, dating consists of pack outings, where small mobs of teens go to movies, hang out at the mall, or play videogames at a friend's house. En masse.

I'm all in favor of girls in groups. Herds are a primitive, but effective, form of self-preservation; strength in numbers is a cliché, but it's also a truism. And I can testify to its effectiveness because it was a tactic deployed against me many times during my campaign to misspend my youth. I'd approach some clearly-out-of-my-league girl at the mall, and a flying wedge of her female companions would appear like the Valkyries and sweep me aside.

So in theory, I'm down with the herd method. But there's one key difference. These dating groups girls travel in today—go to movies with, hang at friends' houses with, *do sleepovers with*—are coed. As in, "Boys included." As in, "The phone call is coming . . . *from inside the house!*"

What now, Liam Neeson? Are you going to tranq-dart your daughter, tag her with an RFID chip, and monitor the movements of the herd? One of the guys in that group could be a high-risk paramour, but how will you know? You can barely keep the names of your kids straight, and now you have to sort out all the Jordans and Parkers and Camerons in your daughter's not-really-dating herd. Heck, you don't even know if the Jordans, Parkers, and Camerons are boys.

And if that's not scary enough, sometimes your kids are dating right in front of you, even if they've *never been on a date*. It's called "d8-ing" and it's a form of online relationship. Here's how the *Wall Street Journal* describes it:

> "Dating" in middle school doesn't mean what many adults think. Tween couples talk mostly via text and chat. Their relationships are fleeting but all-consuming. They date in packs—but expect their boyfriends and girlfriends to be monogamous. And they keep their parents largely in the dark.

Everything from the first "I love you" to the final "I never want to see you again"—all through the ether of the Internet. I'm not sure if this is liberating or terrifying. On the one hand, your children are having their first formative experiences with romance filtered through the tiny screen of an iPhone, which is dehumanizing and terrible. On the other hand, the worst thing that can physically happen to them is a bout of texter's thumb. Nobody needs penicillin for a computer virus. And as for the part about parents being "largely in the dark," well, we guys can live with that, absolutely. But what about us dads?

This is where the guy-versus-dad fault line becomes problematic. As a guy, I really don't want to know what my kids are up to when they're dating. If I found out, I might have to—you know—*do something*. And it would be awfully hypocritical for me—a guy who literally hid in the trunk of a girl's car to get past her protective father—to declare myself Conan the Dad-arian.

Get involved in judging my daughter's dating decisions? The guy part of me just wants to lose myself in an episode of *Game of Thrones* and hope for the best.

It turns out, however, that I really am a dad. I don't just mean that I'm aware of my duties as a father. It's more than that. I've been surprised to discover that just as there is a guy living within me—a relentless advocate for immediate gratification and sexual conquest (though only with my loving wife! Hi, sweetie!)—there's now a protective father inside me, too. It's not a pose. It's an actual part of me, a life-form that sparked into existence the day the doctor put that crying, red-faced girl in my arms. I'm betting you felt that, too. If anything, it would be dishonest and inauthentic of us *not* to play the heavy when it comes to dating.

Now, I have my limits. In 2012 a father in Vermont built a drone that was equipped with a smart phone and video chat. It was designed to follow his kids when they left the house. If you're not comfortable with do-it-yourself surveillance, technology firms will do the work for you. Paranoid parents use cell phones and GPS to plot their kids' movements the way NORAD tracks Russian bombers. Want to know exactly what Wendy is doing on the Web? Products like the iPhone Spy Stic download all of her web traffic, e-mails, and text messages— even the ones she deletes—so you can review them. If you don't want to wait, you can spy on your kids in real time using an innocuous-looking iPhone Dock Camera that recharges your daughter's phone battery while secretly recording what she says and does.

It sounds crazy, constructing a tiny Orwellian surveillance state just for your children. But is it? Lenore Skenazy, the author of *Free-Range Kids* and an opponent of helicopter parenting (so to speak), said of the Drone Dad's device, "I already have an invention that would keep [kids] safe while Dad stays home: It's called 'trust.'" Which is a fine sentiment. Except that it's hard to trust teenagers. They tend to do things to undermine trust, things that often involve motor vehicles, alcohol, and amateur nudity. And besides, is it really a dad's job to trust? Isn't our job to hope for the best, but prepare for the worst?

Because if you pay any attention at all to the popular culture, it sure looks like the worst is out there. Check out Lena Dunham's Twitter timeline, or the average TV sitcom, and you get the sense that, when they're not sexting, our daughters are paying for their cheerleader uniforms by selling their underwear on Craigslist and doing Internet cam shows. It's enough to make a man give up.

Because our kids grow up in a society swamped by the ethos of guy culture, many men come to believe there's no place for dad culture. We're told that hoping the kids date without sex and have sexual self-control is utterly naïve—beyond human capability. Honestly, if you listen to the culture, you get the sense that the father's role is merely to complain about paying for their tramp stamps and then hope the condom doesn't break.

But if you think the fathers have it bad, for the girls it's even worse. Our daughters are under a sexual siege from the moment they wake up until the minute they fall asleep. They have a constant stream of texts and Facebook messages at all hours of the day. They can't get away from would-be paramours, even if they wanted to. And when they aren't under direct assault from the boys, there's a barrage of media messages softening them up as targets. Music, movies, and television offer an all-but-unanimous message: Sex. Now. Yes, *yes*, *YES!* Everybody out there knows that your kids just aren't going to wait.

Except that—this is important—it turns out that everybody is wrong. According to the Guttmacher Institute, most American seventeen-year-olds *haven't* had sex. That's "most," as in, more than half.

In fact, about 40 percent of eighteen-year-olds are virgins, and about a third of nineteen-year-olds are, too. And that trend is getting stronger. The data show that the number of girls reporting that they were sexually active in high school is actually on the decline. A fifteen-year-old girl today is way less likely to be sexually active than she was a generation ago (11 percent versus 20 percent). Perhaps that explains why a 2012 survey of 2,500 college women for a feminist website, HerCampus.com, found that a *majority* of college freshmen were virgins.

These are surveys of large populations of kids from varied backgrounds. Add in other factors, such as being from an intact family or church attendance (both correlate with a delay of sexual activity), and it means that parents who want their kids to "date but wait" have a real chance to help them make that decision. So don't throw in the towel, no matter how much the culture wants you to.

Just so we're clear: This isn't about a mystical obsession with the concept of virginity. It's about wanting better lives for our kids. On this score, the social science is unambiguous: Kids who delay the start of sexual activity and avoid out-of-wedlock pregnancy wind up with better outcomes in just about every area of life—from income to education to personal happiness. There is near-unanimous agreement among researchers that kids dating and learning the ropes of relationships while delaying the sex part is, objectively speaking, a good thing. It's just that everyone assumes that this result is impossible. And again: They're wrong. You can look it up.

So instead of surrender, dads need a strategy for parenting our dating-age kids. I get the sense a lot of guys are working out of the James Bond playbook: Spy on their daughters, track them through social media, get their siblings to flip and become double agents, and if all else fails, tell any boys who come around that if they touch your daughter they'll be shaken, not stirred.

But I'm afraid our mission is much more difficult. We've got to talk to our girls. About girl things.

I know, you'd rather spend a week price-shopping feminine hygiene products with a squad of nuns than have meaningful conversations with your daughter about you-know-what. Relationships, feelings, urges—you don't even talk to your *wife* about that mush, and she regularly sees you naked. Discussing them with your daughter is the stuff of nightmares.

Yet it works. Research shows that it's more often Mom who's talking to teen girls about sex. But that's too bad, because a 2011 study found that "increased father-daughter communication delayed sexual debut." It also found that "responsible sexual behaviors among adolescent females are associated with positive father-daughter communication regarding men, dating, sex, and marriage."

In other words, if you will listen, she will talk.

It's not easy. Talk is not natural guy territory. Men want to *do* things, fix things, have a plan of action. "My daughter wants to start dating?" our male brains think. "Okay—how about a double-date with Mom and Dad?" (Actually proposed by helicopter parents, believe it or not.) "My daughter does her dating en masse? We'll invite the gang to *our* house and break out the Yahtzee and lawn darts." (Again, a true story.)

So what can dads of dating girls *do*? I put that question to a group of about a dozen teenage girls. It was a mixed bunch, ranging in age from middle school to recent college grads. They confirmed that they rarely go on formal dates, that they live their dating lives through their smart phones, and that they *really* hate it when we "creep them on Facebook" (whatever that means). Their unanimous answer to the question of what dads can do to help was . . .

"Nothing."

It turns out that what our kids want from us when they're navigating the uncharted waters of dating and relationships is the same thing they wanted from us when they were presenting their third-grade science projects, and it's what they'll want when we walk them down the aisle. They want us to be the dad. There will always be plenty of guys in their lives—but dads? The strong, reliable, unwavering men who love these young women more than any other man ever will—there will only be one of those.

For teenagers, dating is scary. They need their dads to be scarier. Guys push girls to say "yes." They need to hear Dad's voice saying "no." Most kids are unsure of who they want to be. They need to know that we see the woman they *can* be, and that we will fight for that woman long before she appears.

That's what our daughters need to hear from us. Along with one other thing:

"Keep your pants zipped until you're married!"

As all dads know, you stick with the classics.

CHAPTER 13

College

It's Not as Bad as You Think; It's Worse

Christopher Caldwell

OLD SHANGHAI stood across the street from campus my freshman year. It was the sort of Chinese restaurant you see in those Hollywood movies of the 1930s about rickshaws, tong wars, and opium. They served a punch drink called the Dragon Bucket, basically a quart of rum cut with lemon-lime Kool-Aid, navel-orange wedges, maraschino cherries, and a tray of ice cubes, all sloshed into a ceramic basin like the one my grandmother used for soaking her corns. Each of the boys around the table would get his own long straw and suck the concoction out of the common trough. I say "boys". Alas, girls made up only one-third of the freshman class, and they were already dating upperclassmen. That often left half a dozen of us in the Old Shanghai, lacking anything better to do. One November, at midnight, we decided to climb the church.

There was a nineteenth-century Baptist church a couple hundred yards away. It was crumbling and had been under repair since we arrived. Scaffolding—a rather official-sounding word to describe a few creaking two-by-fours balanced on mildew-covered iron rods—ran eleven stories up to the tip of the black stone steeple. Workmen clambered all over it on weekdays. Jeff Kline was the first of our group to go. There he was, three stories up the scaffold, while the rest of us were still mustering the nerve. As Jeff was hollering down that we should come see how beautiful the city looked, flashing lights appeared. Lots of them. Three squad cars meowed to a stop at the curb.

Jeff was a straight-A student from the Ohio suburbs of Cincinnati. He had probably never exchanged a cross word with a policeman in his life. We had been warned by proctors and counselors at orientation that we ought to obey the campus police (occasionally exasperating) because their job was to protect us from the city police (class-conscious, crime-hardened, thoroughly unpredictable). Here came the city cops now. Jeff looked scared as he descended hand-over-hand. The sergeant, a truculent Boston Irishman, was already wagging his sneering face at Jeff, as if in disbelief and pity.

"Go to school here, son?"

"Yes, sir," Jeff replied.

"You nawmally make a habit of trespassing in houses of wehhhship?"

"No, sir."

"This whatcha fathah's paying five thousand bucks a year faw?"

Jeff paused: "*Ten* thousand bucks," he said. "Sir."

That was a generation ago. Already back then, a year of college cost twice the amount a working-class person considered preposterous—about the price of a big car. Today the cost of private universities has risen to half a dozen times what it was: sixty thousand bucks a year, sometimes more. The price, in certain markets, of a modest house. That adds up to a quarter-million per BA. If your goal in sending your child to university is giving him the wherewithal to stand on his own two feet, you might as well eliminate the middleman and buy him a house outright.

College is both the most important project that upper-middle-class parents and children will ever collaborate on, and the most seemingly irrational. The financial fear it induces has a chilling effect on fecundity: Nobody has extra kids out of a sense that the American university system is a boon. On the contrary. It might well be the most dysgenic social innovation since the invention of priestly celibacy. And there is a mystery at the heart of this exorbitant contrivance: That Irish police sergeant's question, posed back in the days of the Cold War, still has no obvious answer. What *do* fathers think they're paying so many tens of thousands of dollars a year for?

Education, yes. But we seldom agree on what we mean when we say "education." In the most general sense, it's the process of transmitting culture, values, and civilization from parents to children. This process often involves a watershed moment in the life of the youth in question, a moment when he moves from being under the tutelage of adults to dealing with them eye to eye, as comrades and equals. It is usually marked by some rite of passage, the model being the Jewish bar mitzvah. All such rites rest on the idea that there exists lore, writ, and gospel that, while it may not give you all the answers, will at least show you the right way to conduct yourself as you wait to discover the answers.

Religious initiation carries lots of weighty promises that the most up-to-date Americans aren't so sure about anymore. But the very same Americans ingenuously expect those promises to be fulfilled by a humanistic, liberal, secular college education. My father believed this. One of the worst arguments we ever had came the summer before I went off to college. The university had requested a photo for the facebook (in this case, an actual book filled with faces) that would be handed out to the whole freshmen class. My father told me to put on a jacket and tie and comb my hair, and he'd take one of me standing against a blank wall.

"No," I said. This was not a word I used a lot in front of my father, but I wasn't going to look like a doofus.

The problem was that we had two different visions of college. My father looked at it as a destiny, a task, and a privilege. Gestures of respect and even institutional deference were in order. He probably hadn't been any keener to get his picture taken as a freshman at Bowdoin in the 1950s than I was. But he had done it. Back then, one did all that uncomfortable stuff in order to grow into something different: a man.

If I can be blunt about this, perhaps it will explain something about my generation, the last backwash of the baby boom: I wasn't interested in becoming a man. I was interested in becoming a more dashing, brilliant, charismatic, mysterious, attractive-to-girls version of what my suburban, television-age upbringing had turned me into—which was basically a collection of appetites. And there was no way that was going to happen if my official photo showed me dressed up like one of the pallbearers at a farm-town funeral.

So my father and I argued for the reason people usually argue: because we were both right. I was right about the pecking order of my peers. The cold pragmatism of a seventeen-year-old's libido made me an unassailable authority on the subject. My father had a nobler, a more time-honored, and (I would say now) a truer sense of what college was for. But this was a fight that my father could not win, alas, and the now-parents of my own generation appear destined to lose it, too. Father-son arguments today are over different questions than whether a tie makes a young man look like a loser, questions like, "Do you pronounce it 'vaygan' or 'veegan'?" . . . "You mean LGBT like the sandwich?" . . . "What's that in your nose?"

But, today as yesterday, every tool that society has at its disposal is used to prop up the young person's vision of the university as an emancipation, rather than the adult's vision of the university as an inheritance.

This is not an oversight. As they say in Silicon Valley, it's a feature of the university system, not a bug. The modern university is the institution through which the next generation's elite is formed. It inculcates the two essential, nonnegotiable principles of the American ruling class: consumerism and relativism.

The one thing our university system can't countenance is a sturdy, devoutly held system of values that might compete with the established ones. And unfortunately for you, the most likely source of such dangerous values are parents. As such, a main purpose of college is to undermine, and to reverse where possible, the passing on of values from parents to their children. Colleges won't say that out loud, of course. But what they're doing isn't especially new. It's what nineteenth-century ladies' finishing schools and twentieth-century communist training programs once did. In all three cases, the goal of the institution is to set the price of entry into the top social class. (The price is usually steep.)

The experience can feel phony to students and frustrating to parents. College academic programs are a bit like college athletic programs. They are antiquated systems of preparation for professional life that have survived the collapse of their own logic. There is no reason why college athletic departments should serve as the privileged feeders to the NFL and the NBA, especially since this often means a wasteful and humiliating academic charade for young men, ill-suited to it. But there is no reason either why college French, women's studies, or even economics departments should serve as the anteroom to a seven-figure job at Goldman Sachs. The illogic is actually more glaring in the academic case. The Alabama Crimson Tide and the Oregon Ducks make no pretension to attack privilege and battle injustice. Top-flight humanities departments do, and yet their own privileges always go untouched.

Whether or not the parents of college students are paying for an education, they are not *mainly* paying for education. Consider the way colleges have responded to the emerging possibilities of education on the Internet. Yale happily lets Robert Shiller give his course on financial markets on YouTube. Stanford does not object to Sebastian Thrun and Peter Norvig offering their artificial intelligence course, complete with homework assignments, by free video. But if both schools are charging students more than sixty thousand dollars a year while giving away the educational part of their product for free, then what, exactly, are they charging for?

One suspects that the true value-added in their product is the elite credential it offers, and that the credential is more a validation than a qualification. Being shown worthy of admission to a great university impresses people more than anything learned there. Yes, Bill Gates and Mark Zuckerberg dropped out of Harvard before taking their respective degrees. Yet this does not reflect poorly on Harvard; rather the opposite. The institution actually gains prestige so long as people know that it was Harvard the two of them dropped out of.

Alas, this is where discussions about higher education always wind up: Is the university a place to gather professional credentials and expertise (training) or a gentlemanly outlook on the world (education)? These are very different things. The way you bring up your child hinges on your preferences. Most seventeen-year-olds will already have a strong predisposition to one view or the other by the time they start making decisions about college.

In our generation, high-tech moguls and their political apologists have sought to pretend there is no difference between training and education—that this is what Bill Clinton used to call a false choice. "The average eighteen-year-old American will change jobs eight times in a lifetime," President Clinton said when he signed NAFTA in 1993. But this has the ring of propaganda. A twenty-year-old man missing bedtime with his children in order to sit in a junior-college classroom learning to debug some ephemeral software program is not the same as his contemporary who gets to discuss Gibbon at a sherry party. Skilling up so as not to be exploited or pauperized by technological change is not the life of the mind.

Yet the American university system as we know it was founded on this very confusion. When he became president of Harvard in 1869, Charles William Eliot noticed that young men were less interested in knowledge for knowledge's sake than they used (or ought) to be. They wanted a credential in law, medicine, or one of the professions. So Eliot separated the "liberal" arts from "professional" training, requiring the former as a prerequisite for the latter. It has at times been a glorious system. For a century or so it gave us a leadership class that was (for a democracy) highly cultured and (against the odds) a worthy defender of European culture. But that system was totally arbitrary. The illogic of requiring that a young man translate Sappho, memorize Goethe, and know who fought on what side in the Wars of the Roses before he is permitted to try a case in court has grown more and more glaring. Abraham Lincoln would have spent his life tilling the fields if Eliot's system had been in place in his youth.

And anyway, Americans are ambivalent about whether it is better to be a generalist or a specialist. In *The Great Gatsby*, Nick Carraway settles in New York trying to teach himself the bond trade with the help of a dozen books about banking and credit. But he wants more. "I had the high intention of reading many other books besides," he recalls. "I was rather literary in college . . . and now I was going to bring back all such things into my life and become again that most limited of all specialists, the 'well-rounded man.'"

Well-roundedness may seem like a virtue appropriate to the

more class-based society of Fitzgerald's time, when needing to make a living was a sign of low birth. The idea that it constitutes a virtue at all may have something to do with the way ambitious immigrant children of the day were using examination systems to root the children of alumni out of the meritocratic corners of the university system. The term "well-rounded" was meant to introduce arbitrariness into a selection process that had begun to produce results that elites disapproved of. We have our own such terms.

These days college admissions officers profess to want well-roundedness but find themselves dragged into the wider society's quest for "excellence." Parents have made these preferences their own, and now demand from their kids excellence in many things—which is both an impossibility and a great sower of intergenerational tension. In soup kitchens across the country, a familiar sight is the strivers' son, arrived by cab from Dalton, Sidwell Friends, or one of their regional equivalents, spending twenty minutes inattentively ladling out gruel to the destitute, in between studying for tomorrow's Chinese exam and prepping for the debate team. (He got a doctor's note to get out of fencing practice.) His parents have signed him up to "volunteer" so as to demonstrate that he's not all-work-no-play—that he cares. Yeah, he cares. Cares about getting into Duke.

The sentiment that the acquisition of culture is a lifelong adventure, one that can be mixed with a vocation, has endured since the 1960s. It is in most cases a pernicious myth. If you are not a rich genius like Tolstoy, if you are not working as a writer, professor, artist, or scientist, you can, it is true, learn on the job. But it is unlikely to be book learning. People have a hard time acquiring book learning in middle age not because they are deadbeats or philistines, but because it is the human condition. In all societies, the prime of life is a time when people compete with each other to execute projects—and the competition is more intense in our market society. A person in his thirties, forties, or fifties who is still spending part of his time conceptualizing projects (a good description of what education is) will not be able to compete effectively against those who have already done their conceptualizing and can now devote all their energies to executing projects.

This is what Samuel Johnson meant when he told James Boswell of an old man who had warned him, in his own time at Oxford, "Young man, ply your book diligently now, and acquire a stock of knowledge; for when years come upon you, you will find that poring upon books will be but an irksome task." What fortunate parents continue to pay up to a quarter of a million bucks for is an insurance policy against the rainy day when poring upon books becomes irksome. They are buying a space of four adult years when the pressures of earning a living are seemingly (but only seemingly) far off. Those years are for acquiring the lore, writ, and gospel to which, in decades to come, children can turn for guidance, delight, and consolation. Not all kids manage to acquire it. But college is still a bargain for the parents of those who do.

CHAPTER 14

Emerging Adults and Empty Nesters

Just When You Had Fatherhood All Figured Out

Andrew Ferguson

Tocqueville, O Tocqueville, the Ubiquitous, the Inevitable, the Endlessly Quoted and Quotable Tocqueville! It's now 175 years since the French aristocrat traveled the cities and towns and wildernesses of our young country and produced a book—part journalism, part travelogue, part treatise—that is so accurate in its detail and predictions, so pithy and wise, that no gasbag or pseudo-intellectual observer of American life can resist quoting from it.

For instance: me. There I was the other day, reading along in *Democracy in America*, minding my own business, when I fell upon Tocqueville's brief description of how family life fares in a democratic culture, and specifically how young boys somehow manage to become men—rather quickly, as it turns out.

"As soon as the young American approaches manhood," Tocqueville wrote in the late 1830s, "the ties of filial obedience are relaxed day by day: master of his thoughts, he is soon master of his conduct. In America, there is, strictly speaking, no adolescence: at the close of boyhood the man appears, and begins to trace out his own path."

Tocqueville was almost always right—a quality unheard of in a French intellectual, then as now—so I don't doubt that he's accurately describing here the quick transition from boyhood to manhood that was forced upon young men in antebellum America. And from what I can tell, the pattern remained essentially unchanged through the middle years of the last century, with boys going straight to full maturation with no stops in between.

What strikes me about Tocqueville's observation now, though, is how anachronistic it seems, in a book with so few anachronisms. Not only is there, strictly speaking, lots of adolescence in American today, we have a profusion of adolescence, adolescence coming out our ears. Indeed, once begun it seems never to end, at least from a father's point of view. To paraphrase Tocqueville, at the close of boyhood, the man doesn't appear; another boy appears. Except he shaves. And we call him an "emerging adult."

The term *emerging adult* was coined by, who else, a professor of social science in 2000. His name was—is—Jeffrey Jensen Arnett, from Clark University. Arnett points out that while his coinage was new, the phenomenon itself dates at least to the early 1960s. Among the American middle and upper classes, "emerging adulthood" has become a kind of legacy, handed down to the son from the father, who likely spent some time as an emerging adult himself, though he will tend to forget this fact as his son's emergence begins to annoy him. The psychologist Erik Erikson, forty years ago, called this newly invented phase of life "prolonged adolescence." Erikson's tag is less flattering than "emerging adult." It's also more accurate. Arnett prefers to accentuate the positive, however, so his term points to the happy ending, adulthood, rather than the problematic aimlessness in the middle.

As Arnett defines them, emerging adults are between eighteen and twenty-nine. They are footloose and fancy free. Their emergence begins when they leave home after high school for college—a large majority of high school graduates in the United States now go on to some kind of higher education—and there, assuming campus is more than a half-day's walk from their parents' house, they are left to their own devices. Colleges and universities long ago abandoned the parietal rules that allowed administrators to serve as monitors of behavior in the absence of Mom and Dad. After a few years filled with daily and nightly parties, occasional classes, and sexual encounters ranging in number from a fumbling handful to staggering, JFK-like excess, our emerging adults escape from college, usually unmarried and unattached, bearing a mixture of ambitions—professional and personal, all of them half-baked—and muddle through the next few years until marriage and a career claim them and, we're supposed to hope, tame them.

Emerging adulthood, Arnett wrote in his big academic paper on the subject, "is a time of frequent change as various possibilities in love, work, and worldviews are explored." Isn't that sweet?

It is typical of our polite, judgment-free way of talking that we should refer to a decade of screwing around as a "period of exploration," but then we also insist on referring to our teenage enthusiasm for smoking dope at every given chance as "experimenting with marijuana." It makes us sound like we're all members of the Shackleton expedition, or Madame Curie. Not quite, though. From many years of surveys and interviews, Arnett and other psychologists and anthropologists have tried to get a handle on what makes "emerging adulthood" distinctive for the average American. They conclude that there isn't much distinctive about it—which makes it distinctive, if you see what I mean.

Unlike other discrete life phases that social scientists like to isolate and define, in which certain traits and conditions are widely shared among a cohort, nothing about emerging adulthood is "normative demographically." For instance, we can easily describe the life of adolescents—kids under eighteen and over eleven. They live at home; almost none of them are married; almost all of them go to school; hardly any of them have kids of their own. Once across the threshold of eighteen, however, the picture breaks up. Emerging adults live all over the place; a lot of them are married, most aren't; some have kids, most don't; some are in school, some in the workforce, some slog through both at the same time; and so on. All they have in common, aside from chronological age, is that they're too much like adults to be called kids and too childlike to be called adults.

Fifty years ago, most men got married at twenty-two or younger; for women the median age was twenty. Today the numbers are twenty-nine and twenty-seven, and they're rising. Similar postponements can be seen in choosing a career. A decision likely to be made at the age of twenty-two a half century ago is now delayed, more often than not, to the late twenties or beyond. Erikson watched as this prolonged adolescence was taking shape in American culture, and he wasn't sure he liked what he saw. Too stern for polite talk—he was a refugee from Nazism—he called this period a "psychosocial moratorium" from the business of life, and there's an unmistakable note of disapproval in the phrase. A moratorium, after all, is what happens when we stop doing what we are supposed to be doing.

Arnett, on the other hand, is a thoroughly modern social observer in the commercial mode, tracking the footsteps of such successful, well-compensated popularizers as Malcolm Gladwell, Dan Ariely, and Jonah Lehrer. He has turned his research into a kind of cottage industry, publishing books and writing magazine articles and giving speeches on emerging adulthood. Like everyone in the social-observer racket, he knows that if he fails to flatter his audience, or if they sense the slightest whiff of Eriksonian disapproval of their "life choices," they won't buy his books or watch his TED talks or read his magazine articles, and he will wind up a very unsuccessful, not at all well-compensated, social observer indeed.

His picture of the emerging adult is therefore generally rosy, and definitely nonjudgmental. (We are judgmental only toward judgmental people.) In tracing the inspiration for the rise of emerging adulthood, he lands upon the most obvious answer: We do it because we can. This years-long vacation from the rigors of life, this reluctance on the part of a young man to settle down until all other possibilities have been exhausted—this indulgence is made possible only by the mind-boggling affluence of highly developed Western economies. Any country that can turn playing badminton, walking dogs, and teaching journalism into paying jobs is not merely swimming in surplus wealth; it will have enough left over to sustain a cohort of tens of millions of less-than-productive twenty-five-year-olds as they discover when, where, how, and whether they will someday become productive.

Surveys of emerging adults suggest that something else is going on, too, beyond the laxity that vast wealth can buy. Emerging adults define adulthood in ways that wouldn't have occurred to their grandparents, much less to Tocqueville's nineteenth-century families. Two generations ago a person was thought to have grown up when he passed certain visible markers on life's path—by keeping a steady job, mastering a sellable skill, earning a college degree, getting married, providing for children, buying a house. An adult was defined by what an adult did.

Emerging adults, by contrast, tell Arnett and other researchers that an adult is defined by how he feels about himself. Do we have a positive self-concept? Do we make decisions independently? Do we "take responsibility" for our actions, whatever that may mean? These are subjective questions, of course, answerable only by the subject himself, which serves to keep any judgmental second-guessers at bay. An emerging adult is an adult when he feels himself to be one. Thus can a thirty-year-old man tell himself he's a fully formed adult even as he lives with his mother—even as she does his laundry twice a week, even as she makes him peanut butter and banana sandwiches with the crusts trimmed off. The day his self-concept feels solid is the day he can stand tall: Today I am a man.

Or if not today, then tomorrow for sure. And Mom will agree. Bless her heart.

And what *about* Mom? And Dad, for that matter? Arnett's surveys and others show that parents who think the "longer road to adulthood" is a bad idea outnumber those who don't by more than three to one. And no wonder: Three out of four parents of emerging adults say they're providing them with some measure of financial assistance. A shorter road to adulthood would surely be less expensive for all concerned. Yet in consolation, parents are expected to enjoy their own psychosocial moratorium at the same time that their pupal semi-adults are busy, or not, emerging. All the signals sent by our cultural authorities, from Oprah and Katie to Ellen and Matt Lauer, tell us so. Parents of emerging adults are supposed to be frolicking in the empty nest.

Unlike *emerging adult*, the origins of the phrase *empty nest* are lost in the misty bogs where journalism mingles with social science. It is most often bundled with the ugly word *syndrome*, which gives the phrase in its entirety a split personality, at once cozy and clinical. Not everybody likes it. Over the last twenty years or so, many feminists have objected to the term "empty-nest syndrome" as both ageist and sexist. It "perpetuates the language of the barnyard" to describe women, as one offended scholar wrote. An empty nest might once have been home to birds and chicks, or serve as the current perch of an old hen. The scholars recommend the substitute term "postparental period," which, for all its admirable alliteration, is too plain as well as inaccurate: There is no such period. Parents never get over being parents.

Which is why our social scientists have identified the syndrome. It was originally meant to describe an emotionally and spiritually perilous time when men and women who have consumed themselves for twenty or thirty years in the demands of parenthood suddenly find themselves bereft—of children, of course, but also of the kid-related preoccupations around which a certain kind of parent builds his life. I can testify to the peril, if the reader will indulge a personal note, for I am that kind of parent. At first, my wife and I confronted a *half*-empty nest. My son was off to college as my daughter remained behind, but with his absence I had the sense of an irreversible change in our circumstances, a preliminary hollowing out that awaited only her departure, a year hence, to complete.

I had been a big fan of fatherhood, believing it to be the only incontestably important task a man is given to perform in life, and as the kids departed and the demands seeped away I felt the loss, actual and prospective, as a physical thing, a hitch in my muscle memory. For many years it had fallen to me to help make them breakfast. Now this routine, impressed into me at the cellular level through constant repetition, was confounded.

In the early morning hours, as the children watched, I had worked with balletic efficiency, positioning myself light-footed near the island in mid-kitchen, able to reach far enough to plunge the bread in the toaster and yet swing around to open the refrigerator door with one hand and withdraw the orange juice with the other before hooking my right foot around the door to slam it shut, using the torque generated thereby to reach high for the juice glasses and then slide down the island bent low to the shelf where the lunchboxes were stacked, which

I brought up and placed, assembly-line fashion, across from the refrigerator where the fixings for lunch lay waiting . . . and waiting . . . for now I stood useless in our half-empty nest, planted lead-footed in the kitchen near the island, as my daughter, uninterested in breakfast, brushed by.

"Useless" is the key word here. There is a sense of diminished utility. It increases when the children settle themselves in college and then only more so when the college years end and the most burdensome financial obligations (tuition bills) cease and the young adults begin emerging. In time I grew unsettled enough that I consulted the empty-nest literature, which is vast: *Empty Nest: How to Have Fun; The Empty Nest: Finding Hope; Empty Nest: A Mother's Hidden Grief; The Empty Nest Chronicles;* and even this, the bible of denial and a pathetic cry for help: *My Nest Isn't Empty.*

We baby boomers have marked each stage of life's "journey" by burying it in a lava flow of books like these, books about what we're doing, have done, should do. Large as it is, the empty-nest literature isn't as vast as the birthing literature that my wife and I had consulted before our first child was born, though it was more numerous than the books we had acquired as he approached the terrible twos, which were matched in number by the books we read in preparing him for grade school, and then the next set for high school and the angst of the teenage years. I pushed aside the towering piles of college admissions books we'd bought six years ago to make room for the empty-nest books, which now line up next to the books I have bought about my emerging adults.

And that's when I discovered that "empty-nest syndrome," originally conceived as a time of anxiety and unease, had been recast by dint of unconquerable American cheerfulness into a period of constant pleasure—as experimental and exploring as emerging adulthood. The two phases, empty nest and emerging adulthood, have taken their place as the bookends of life for the American middle and upper classes. The tone brought to both is relentlessly upbeat, ticking off the things you can do that are much more fun than the humdrum obligations of life. "Don't get trapped in sad!" I read. "You have a new life to create. Make it glorious, fulfilling, and fun-filled." "You've created the perfect child," one "life coach" wrote. (How did he know?) "Now go and create your perfect life."

It seems we have no other choice. "Revel in your new role," wrote another psychologist. "Watch movies until 4:00 a.m., eat cereal for dinner, invite friends over midweek." Nothing would trap me in sad like eating cereal for dinner, but that's just the beginning. I was told to learn to play the piano, to become proficient in pottery making, and to write poetry in a new language. And in every article and book and PBS pledge-drive special there was the familiar suggestion of sexual abandon: Life as a Cialis ad. "Your house will be yours again, to use as you wish . . . at all hours . . . without worries of being interrupted . . ." (nudge-nudge, wink-wink). The popular Huffington Post website even offered an alphabetized guide to life in the empty nest, and the infantilization seemed appropriate. "K is for kick ass, as in 'empty nesting can be kick-ass fun.'" J is for "jump start your sex life." L is, of course, for "lust . . . feeling it again in an empty house." Z is for "zone . . . erogenous." S, incredibly, is only for "sleep." Everybody must be all tuckered out.

We are deep into another psychosocial moratorium of the kind that Erikson disapproved of, although *holiday* might be the more appropriate word, given the cheerfulness with which we are supposed to embrace it. And lovely as they seem, taken one by one, these two newly discovered phases of life—unknown to our grandparents, conjured up from the deadly combination of runaway affluence and social scientists eager to find something to study—seem more disconcerting when you do the math. If a young person isn't expected to get serious until he's twenty-nine, and then he gets to knock off to create his perfect life when his kids leave home—when he's fifty-five, let's say—there's not much time left in between for him to get any actual work done. Assuming a life expectancy of eighty, together the two holidays constitute two-thirds of the span from cradle to grave.

This is nice work if you can get it. And it does no good to bemoan it—our national flaccidity, our disinclination to buckle down, as earlier generations would have said. We'd do better to close on an upbeat note ourselves, by noting that empty nesting and emerging adulthood aren't the only innovations in family life that America has offered the world. There is another innovation that has been, and will continue to be, pleasing to fathers and sons alike. For in America, as his children grow older,

> The father exercises no other power than that with which men love to invest the affection and the experience of age; his orders would perhaps be disobeyed, but his advice is for the most part authoritative. Though he be not hedged in with ceremonial respect, his sons at least [approach] him with confidence; no settled form of speech is appropriated to the mode of addressing him, but they speak to him constantly, and are ready to consult him day by day; the master and the constituted ruler have vanished— the father remains.

Take heart, then: the Father remains. Or so wrote Tocqueville, and he knew his stuff.

CHAPTER 15

Love and Marriage

*How to Talk to Your Kids about the Most
Important Decision They'll Ever Make*

Rob Long

A SON ONCE ASKED his father to explain what marriage was like. His father answered by taking the son's iPod, removing every song but his son's current favorite, and handing it back to him. "That, kid," his father said, "is what it's like to be married. So before you get married, better ask yourself, *Is this my favorite song?*"

Which is, when you get right down to it, the gist. You can only listen to one song for the rest of your life, but it's your favorite song, so it's okay. Or, if you're not ready to make that kind of commitment, you can keep listening to all of those other songs, skipping happily from track to track, as long as you're prepared never to listen to your favorite song again.

I'm not sure I would have put the matter exactly that way if asked by my own son. But then, I'm what you might call a disinterested expert in the fields of marriage and fatherhood because of my current (and likely future) status as an unmarried and childless male. Which means that, like Dr. Jane Goodall among the chimpanzees in Africa, I have a unique vantage point on the institution of marriage.

"The problem with women," said a friend of mine who is married to a stubborn woman, "is that they're all so stubborn."

"Guys are stupid," said a woman I know from college who is married to a stupid man.

You see, like the good ol' Dr. Jane, I don't have a chimp in the fight, which means I'm able to think about marriage from a neutral perspective. Unburdened from the specifics of a particular relationship—but often given an awkward front-row seat to the marriages of my friends—I can watch and take field notes and pass silent judgment on the mistakes and missteps of my married friends. And then pass on my wisdom to you and your spawn.

And no, the judgment is not *always* silent.

A few years ago, I was visiting some friends who were living, temporarily, in Paris. They were a young couple with a newborn, living in a small apartment in the 7th arrondissement—and if you just read those words and thought, *Wow, that sounds romantic and glamorous*, then you are clearly unmarried and childless and need to read on. Because, as often happens at moments like this, when everything is supposed to be infused with joy and wonder, they were stressed and sleep-deprived and fighting a lot.

In other words, it was a perfect time to visit.

The husband was an old friend of mine, and one afternoon we were tasked with taking the baby out for a bit. His wife needed a nap and some time alone, and the idea was that he would walk the few short blocks to my hotel and we would sit in the warm lobby—this was February, when Paris is particularly cold and damp—and after an hour or two he would report back to headquarters with the bundle of warm baby, returning her in roughly the same condition in which he checked her out.

"Make sure she has her hat," his wife told him. "It's too cold for her little head. Just sit in the lobby. Make sure she's warm. Make sure you take the blanket. Make sure you. . . ."

And what followed, I suspect, was a litany of *make sures* and *don'ts* including, I'm fairly certain, a specific instruction not to take the baby outside for a walk in the Paris winter, despite the fact that the day was sunny and dry, despite the fact that strolling the Paris boulevards is an ancient and lordly practice, despite the fact that Cuban cigars are legal in France and that I had two of them and that nothing could be better than sauntering up to the *Jardin du Luxembourg* with the little baby in the *poussette* and lighting up like gentlemen. And despite the fact that we did just that and, boy, let me tell you, was she mad.

Like, volcanic mad.

Apparently, anyway. I was safely in my hotel room. Or maybe out and about, drinking heavily without consequence, as is my prerogative as a childless, unmarried male who will die alone.

"She's still furious," he told me the next day. "She's using all those words they use. I 'disrespected' her. I treated her with 'disdain' and 'dismissal.' I 'arrogated'—is that even a word?— to myself the right to make 'unilateral' decisions about our child."

"So what did you do?" I asked as I broke into my croissant and sipped my *café crème*.

"I apologized, and apologized, and blamed you."

"Hmmm. Probably a good move," I said. "But wait. How is what you did 'disrespectful'? I mean, did she *ask* your opinion about what to do with the baby? Did you guys come to a *consensus?*"

"No," he said, eyes widening a little. "She just gave me orders."

"Well," I said, "talk about unilateral! Talk about disrespect! Talk about arrogating—and yes, it is a word—the right to make childcare decisions!"

"You're right!" he shouted. And went back to the apartment to renew the battle, which reignited and fizzled and reignited and fizzled over several years—at different provocations—and ended, eventually, in divorce.

Which was not—despite what I know you're thinking—my fault. Although you'd be right to point out that Dr. Jane Goodall only rarely gave the chimpanzees relationship advice.

I once met a man who had pioneered a new way to teach English to foreigners. English can be a baffling and irrational language to newcomers. Our grammar is a landmine of contradictions and special cases; our spelling is a chaotic mishmash of dozens of other languages; and our rules of pronunciation are considered, in some university faculties, complex to the point of racism.

So how did he do it? How did he manage to reengineer the teaching of English as a second language?

Simple, he said. "My feeling is," he told me, "that everyone is basically a foreigner. My kids are foreigners. My coworkers are foreigners. My *wife* is a foreigner. They all speak their own weird language. So when you realize that no one is really speaking the same language, it's a lot easier to come up with ways to bridge that. It's not about English or Japanese or Swahili. It's about this person in his or her own head thinking they're making sense when actually you have zero idea what they're saying."

Which, along with the one-song iPod, is another way to explain the challenges of marriage.

What my friend, years ago in Paris, didn't realize—and what I didn't either, but then, I didn't need to—was that his wife wasn't expressing actual rational concern about the weather and the baby and the dangers of the *Jardin du Luxembourg*. What she was expressing was the very real and natural reaction many women have after the birth of their first child: fear that something awful is about to happen; guilt at every moment spent not transfixed with the baby's physical presence; a sense that this precious object that was so recently tucked safely inside her is now outside and helpless and unprotected.

That catechism of *don'ts* and *make sures* was in a foreign language, and the translation was, "I'm really terrified about this, about being a mother, about being tired, about failing at this job before I've even really done it." His job, as a husband, was to do his best to hear what she was saying in her (maybe crazy) language, understand it, accept it, and turn to his friend with the cigars and say, in language unprintable in this volume, please stop talking, we're not leaving this lobby, this is just the way it is, please stop talking.

So, after you hand the one-song iPod back to your kid and tell him (or her) that marriage is like one of those Andrew Lloyd Webber musicals where it's one song, over and over again, at differing volumes, maybe also add this:

Ask yourself: Can you learn the personal and nutty language your intended insists on using? Not—and this is a crucial distinction—can you *teach* your intended to speak your language. But can you learn what she means when she says, "Take a blanket." Or what he means when he says, "I don't know what to do about this Amex bill." Because from my vantage point, looking through a telescope at the community of chimpanzees, all trying to make their marriages work and thrive, when you know what your partner means—really means—you can get through anything. And when you don't, you can't get through a simple disagreement about a walk in the park.

And it really doesn't matter if you love each other.

"Love," says the Apostle Paul in 1 Corinthians 13, "never fails."

My guess is, had he known that this particular passage of scripture would be legally required at every single wedding ceremony—along with Etta James's "At Last" and some awkward intergenerational dancing—he might have gone straight from 1 Corinthians 11 ("Everyone who is hungry should eat something at home") to 1 Corinthians 14 ("Now, brothers and sisters, if I come to you and speak in tongues, what good will I be to you, unless I bring you some revelation or knowledge or prophecy or word of instruction?") without taking the troublesome and difficult detour to love.

That's what your kid will want to know, when you tell him or her about the iPod and the foreign-language thing. The kid will want to know about love, which—sorry, Paul—fails so regularly and so spectacularly that the Letter to the Corinthians should come with a release form.

There once was a young couple who loved each other very much. (This is a true story, despite the rather unbelievable opening.)

They had an expensive and elaborate wedding planned in a swank location in San Francisco. About an hour before the ceremony, the bride and her party were in their gigantic hotel suite preparing for the event—there were makeup artists and photographers and dressers and minions circling around—and one of the bridesmaids—the one none of them will ever speak to again, probably—was looking around for a place to hang her outfit when she had an idea.

With a piece of string, she fashioned a makeshift clothesline from one side of the room to the other, attaching the string to the fire sprinklers which were (unusually, but there you have it) along the side wall.

Do you see where this is going? She somehow wrapped one end of the string around the little doo-dad inside the sprinkler housing that trips the fire alarm, so when one of the other bridesmaids tugged a little too hard on the string, the alarm went off. Which made three things occur:

First, a heavy, black, fire-retardant powder sprayed all over the room from multiple ceiling vents. Then the sprinklers went off. Then everything was covered in black mud. Then everyone was screaming. (Okay, that's four things. But two of them happened at the same time.) All of the gowns were ruined. All of the hairdos were collapsed and wet. All of the women were streaked with tears and black soot. It was like Prom Night at Goth High. The hysterical bride picked up the phone and called the groom and wailed out her news.

Let's hit Pause. Pretend you're the handsome groom. What would you do? Think about it. Expensive wedding. Expensive gowns. Church filling up with people. Stores closed. Weeping bride. This is a testing moment.

Here's what he did: He called down to the concierge and asked for help. He explained the situation and together they tracked down someone at the local fancy department store and managed to cobble together some wedding attire, and they pulled off the wedding, a mere two hours late.

At the reception, making the traditional groom's toast, he told the story—now, hours later, crisis over, it was sort of funny and charming—and swaggered a bit. *I got it done*, he wanted everyone to know. *I'm a young man who executes the mission*, his beaming smile seemed to say. And his bride beamed, too. *My husband saved the wedding.*

"For a minute," he said, "what I was going to do was come down to my wife's room and tell her to put on some jeans and scoop her up and bring her to the church. Because it doesn't matter to me what she wears. And I would have said to you all right then and there to imagine her in the most beautiful gown in the world, looking like the most beautiful woman on earth, because that's what I see every time I look at her."

Most of the guests swooned a bit. There was applause, there were some tears, but I couldn't help but notice—it's my job, after all, to keep an eye on the chimpanzee who isn't talking— the smile on the bride's face change a bit when she heard what dashing and romantic thing her husband *almost* did, what his heroic and manly impulse *almost* was, before he squashed it and called the concierge and got them to call the lady to open the Saks.

Hours after her marriage ceremony, the bride learned a new and disappointing thing about her groom: He knew the right thing to do but would not do it. Love never fails, except when it does. Except when it thinks twice, gets sensible, and calls downstairs for help.

By now, of course, any reasonable child will regret ever asking you about marriage. All you'll have said—aside from referring, inexplicably, to an outdated MP3 player—is that it's important to listen, and if you're thinking about doing something bold and romantic, do it, or don't do it—but if you don't do it, then shut up about it. You'll have said some disparaging things about love—and maybe, if you're the father of a potential bride, saved yourself some money on a pricey hotel suite by reminding her that they don't have those tricky sprinklers at the Days Inn—but what you won't have done is answered the big question, which is: How do I know?

How do I know this is the one for me? Because despite the divorce rate—which, it needs to be said, is flattening—people go into this thing with the thought that it's forever. I've been to dozens of weddings—I've even officiated at one—and I've never heard vows that included the phrase, "You know, we'll see how it goes," or "We're going to play this thing by ear."

The young person who's looking to you for advice, to explain this mysterious institution that tests our patience and practicality (and one to which some of us have wisely opted out and others have unwisely tried and been ejected), is looking for what every young person is looking for these days, and that's a trick that makes the whole thing simpler and cleaner. A way to know for sure that the boyfriend or girlfriend deserves, as they say on the Facebook, a relationship status upgrade.

When your kid asks this question, there's only one thing to do. Put him or her in the car and drive to Starbucks.

Not just any Starbucks. Pick one in a suburban or exurban area—something surrounded by nice neighborhoods and good schools and well-kept roads and parkways. Go in the middle of a weekday, when kids are in class and the place is filled with grown-ups. Stand there, somewhere around the case of sweet carbohydrates and the bins of water, and point out who's there.

I'll tell you who will be there (it's who's always there): a lot of middle-aged guys sitting alone at tables with big Dell laptops opened up to their LinkedIn profiles. They've got their phones plugged in to a power strip they brought with them, a venti latté and a lemon pound cake slice at hand, and they're sending out e-mails and updating their résumés and networking and paddling furiously along because life, at their age, has gotten very hard.

The middle-aged dudes at the local Starbucks are out of work, but they'll call themselves "consultants," and they'll mean it, too. They'll be consulting here and there—for local merchants or friends-of-friends—and doing whatever it is they can do to catch up to an economy that seems to be moving just a little faster than they can run along behind it. When the financial system went bananas a few years ago and the country's economic engine sputtered to a crawl, a lot of those middle-aged guys got caught on the wrong side of the ledger. At one point or another, in all of our lives—man or woman, young or old, married or single—we're that guy at Starbucks. We're sitting there with the unfashionable laptop just trying to make something happen.

Now, the young person in your life won't really believe this will happen to them—that's part of being young, of course. But seeing the Men of Starbucks in person, seeing their dogged tapping and scrolling and the way they gin up a cheerful and optimistic tone to answer and place calls—"Hey, Steve, this is Doug, just giving you a shout back in regards to the e-mail I sent last week, hoping you've had a chance to look it over and that we can discuss it at your convenience. Happy to talk anytime. Take care . . ." —well, I suspect it will make an impression on them nonetheless.

So tell them this: We will all—you can count on it—be lost in the Starbucks Wilderness in our lives. We will all—you can count on it—lose jobs and run low on confidence and feel like we missed the magic express train that everyone else caught. And when that happens, ask yourself: Will there be someone in my life who knows me, knows how hard I'm trying, knows that I'm scared about the baby and about money and about us and about everything?

And—equally important—will I know that about someone else? Is it the person across from me right now? Is it my boyfriend who doesn't always listen or my girlfriend who has annoying friends? When I'm here having my metaphorical Starbucks moment, who do I want in my corner, sending me encouraging texts and cheerful emoticons?

When the Men of Starbucks pack up their laptops and toss their napkins and head out into the night, there's only one thing that will make them feel strong and loved and ready to try again, and that's their favorite song.

Just that one song.

CHAPTER 16

Thanks, Grandpa
Grandfatherhood and the Spirit of the Age
Joseph Epstein

As with lengths of skirts, lapels on men's suits, breast-feeding, and other more or less important customs, there are also fashions in fatherhood. The institution changes from generation to generation. As a man of *un age certain*—if numbers be wanted, mine is seventy-eight—my experience of fatherhood, both from the receiving and giving end, is likely to be different from those of younger contributors to this august volume.

I had the good fortune to have an excellent father. He was fair, utterly without neuroses, a model of probity, honorable in every way. Born in Canada, my father departed Montreal to make his fortune in Chicago at the age of seventeen, without bothering to finish high school. Until his forties, when he came to own his own business, he was a salesman, but without any of the slickness or slyness usually associated with the occupation. He made his sales by winning over customers through his amiability, his reliability, and the utter absence of con in his presentation. He was successful, and became rich enough, in Henry James's phrase, "to meet the demands of his imagination," which weren't extravagant.

When, at the age of eighteen, it was time for me to go to college, my father told me that he would of course pay for my college education, but since I had shown so little interest in school, he wondered if I wouldn't do better to skip college. He thought that I would make a terrific salesman. This, you have to understand, was intended as a serious compliment; one of two I remember his paying me. The other came years later and had to do with my taking care of a complicated errand for him. After I had accomplished what he wanted me to do, he said, "You handled that in a very businesslike way."

If this sounds as if I am complaining, the grounds being emotional starvation from want of approval, be assured that I'm not. Approval wasn't an item high on the list of emotional expenditure in our family. (When in my early thirties I informed my mother that I, who had no advanced degrees, had been offered a job teaching at Northwestern University, she replied, "That's nice, a job in the neighborhood," and we went on talk of other things.) I cannot ever recall seeking my parents' approval; it was only their disapproval that I wished to avoid, and this because it might cut down on my freedom, which, from an early age, was generous and extensive.

The not-especially-painful truth is that my brother and I— and I believe this is true of many families of our generation— were never quite at the center of our parents' lives. Their own lives—rightly, I would say—came first. So many in my generation, I have noticed, were born five or six years apart from our next brother or sister. The reason for this is that parents of that day decided that raising two children born too close together was damned inconvenient. The standard plan was to wait until the first child was in school before having a second.

My parents were never other than generous to my brother and to me. They never knocked us in any way. We knew we could count on them. But we also knew they had lives of their own and that we weren't, as is now so often the case with contemporary parents, everything to them. My mother had her charities, her card games, her friends. My father had his work, where he was happiest and most alive.

My father's exalted status as a breadwinner was central to his position in our household. The breadwinning function of men in those days, when so few married women worked, was crucial. Recall what a dim figure Pa Joad, in John Steinbeck's *The Grapes of Wrath*, is; the reason is that he is out of work, without financial function, and so the leadership in the novel is ceded to Ma Joad, the mother and dominant figure in the family. Although my father was the least tyrannical of men, my mother felt that he was owed many small services. "Get your father's slippers," my mother would say. "Ask your father if he'd like a glass of water." We were instructed not to "rumple up the newspaper before your father comes home."

As a Canadian, my father had no interest in American sports, so he never took my brother and me to baseball or football games. (He did like boxing, and on a couple of occasions he and I went to watch Golden Gloves matches together.) He certainly never came to watch me play any of the sports in which I participated. But then, in those days, no father did; his generation of fathers were at work—my father worked six days a week—and had no time to attend the games of boys. (I'm talking about presoccer days, and so girls in those days played no games.) Nor would it ever have occurred to me to want my father to watch me at play. One of the fathers among my friends did show up for lots of his son's games and was mocked behind his back for doing so; a Latinist among us referred to him as Omnipresent.

Although my father did not take me to sports or other events, or attend my own games, I nevertheless spent lots of time with him. From the age of fifteen through twenty, I drove with him to various midwestern state fairs, where he sold costume jewelry to concessionaires. I was, officially, his flunky, schlepping his sample case and doing most of the driving. We shared hotel rooms. What amazes me now that I think about those many hours we spent together is how little of that time was given to intimate conversation between us. I never told my father about my worries, doubts, or concerns, nor did he tell me his. We never spoke about members of our family, except, critically, of dopey cousins or older brothers of his who had gone astray. We talked a fair amount about his customers. He offered me advice about saving, the importance of being financially independent, about never being a show-off of any kind—all of it perfectly sound advice, if made more than a touch boring by repetition.

Neither of us, my father or I, craved intimacy with the other. I wouldn't have known how to respond to an invitation to intimacy from him. I would have been embarrassed if he had told me about any of his weaknesses or deep regrets. So far as I could surmise, he didn't have any of either. Since I was a small boy I recall his invocation, often repeated, "Be a man." A man, distinctly, did not reveal his fears, even to his father; what a man did with his fears was conquer them.

The generation of my father—men born in the first decade of the twentieth century, who came into their maturity during the Depression—was distinctly prepsychological. In practice, this meant that such notions as insecurity, depression, or inadequacy of any sort did not signify as anything more than momentary lapses to be overcome by hitching up one's trousers and getting back to work. My father and I did not hug, we did not kiss, we did not say "I love you" to each other. This may seem strangely distant, even cold to a generation of huggers, sharers, and deep-dish carers. No deprivation was entailed here, please believe me. We didn't *have* to do any of these things, my father and I. The fact was, I loved my father, and I knew he loved me.

By the time I had children of my own, psychology had

conquered with strong repercussions for child rearing. Benjamin Spock's book *Baby and Child Care* (1946), said in its day to be, after the Bible, the world's second-best-selling book, had swept the boards. Freudian theory was still in its ascendance. Under the new psychological dispensation, children were now viewed as highly fragile creatures, who if not carefully nurtured could skitter off the rails into a life of unhappiness and failure. As a young father, I was not a reader of Spock, nor was I ever a Freudian, yet so pervasive were the doctrines of Spock and Freud that their influence was unavoidable.

I was not a very good father; measured by current standards, I may have been a disastrous one. Having divorced from their mother when my sons were ten and eight years old, and having been given custody of them, I brought to my child rearing a modest but genuine load of guilt. I do not have any axiomatic truths about raising children except this one: Children were meant to be brought up by two parents. A single parent, man or woman, no matter how extraordinary, will always be insufficient.

Children, according to Dr. Spock and Dr. Freud, needed to be made to feel secure and loved. I couldn't do much about the first. But I proclaimed my love a lot to my sons, so often that they must have doubted that I really meant it. "You know I love you, goddamnit," I seem to recall saying too many times, especially after having blown my cool by yelling at them for some misdemeanor or other. Thank goodness I had boys; girls, I have discovered, cannot be yelled at, at least not with the same easy conscience.

Fortunately, my sons were fairly tough and independent characters. Neither of them as kids was interested in sports, so I didn't have to attend their Little League games. I took only a modest interest in their schooling. (My parents took none whatsoever in mine, which, given my wretched performance in school, was a break.) Nor did I trek out to Disneyland with them. My sons spent their Sundays with my parents, and my father, who turned out to be a fairly attentive grandfather, took them to the Museum of Science and Industry, the Adler Planetarium, the Shedd Aquarium, and other museums around Chicago. Raising children as a single parent, much of life during those years is now in my memory a blur—a blur of vast loads of laundry, lots of shopping, and less than first-class cookery (mine). "Dad, this steak tastes like fish," I remember one of my sons exclaiming, a reminder that I needed to do a better job of cleaning the broiler.

My oldest son, unlike his father, was good at school. When he was in high school he took to playing rock at a high volume in his room. I asked him how he could study with such loud music blaring away. "I seem to be getting all A's, Dad," he said. "Are you sure you want me to turn the music down?" He went on to Stanford, my other son to the University of Massachusetts. I drove neither of them on what is now the middle-class parents' compulsory tour of campuses while their children are in their junior year of high school. Nor did I tell them to which schools to apply. What I said is that I would pay all their bills, that I didn't need to look at their course selection or care about their major or grades, but only asked that they not make me pay for courses in science fiction or in which they watched movies. I visited each of them once while he was in college. I pasted no college decals on the back window of my car.

Some unknown genius for paradox said, "Married, single—neither is a solution." A similar formulation might be devised for the best time to have children: in one's twenties, thirties, forties, beyond—none seems ideal. In my generation, one married young—in my case, at twenty-three—and had children soon thereafter. The idea behind this was to become an adult early, and thereby assume the responsibilities of adulthood: wife, children, house, dogs, "the full catastrophe," as Zorba the Greek put it. Now nearly everyone marries later, and women often delay having children, whether married or not, until their late thirties, sometimes early forties.

In one's twenties, one has the energy, but usually neither the perspective nor the funds, to bring up children with calm and understanding. Later in life, when one is more likely to have the perspective and the funds, the energy has departed. In my own case, along with having children to take care of, I had my own ambition with which to contend. I worked at forty-hour-a-week jobs, wrote on weekends and early in the mornings before work, read in the evenings, picked up socks and underwear scattered around the apartment, took out garbage, and in between times tried to establish some mild simulacrum of order in the household.

Because of this hectic life, my sons got less attention but more freedom than those of their contemporaries who had both parents at home; and vastly more freedom than kids brought up during these past two decades when the now-still-regnant, child-centered culture has taken over in American life in a big way.

I have a suspicion that this cultural change began with the entrée into the language of the word "parenting." I don't know the exact year that the word "parenting" came into vogue, but my guess is that it arrived around the same time as the new full-court press, boots-on-the-ground-with-heavy-air-support notion of being a parent. To be a parent is a role; parenting implies a job. It is one thing to be a parent, quite another to parent. "Parenting (or child rearing) is the process of promoting and supporting the physical, emotional, social, and intellectual development of a child from infancy to adulthood. Parenting refers to the aspects of raising a child aside from the biological relationship," according to the opening sentence of the

Wikipedia entry on the subject. Read further down and you will find dreary paragraphs on "parenting styles," "parenting tools," "parenting across the lifespan," and more, alas, altogether too much more.

Under the regime of parenting, raising children became a top priority, an occupation before which all else must yield. The status of children inflated greatly. Much forethought went into giving children those piss-elegant names still turning up everywhere: all those Brandys and Brandons and Bradys; Hunters, Taylors, and Tylers; Coopers, Porters, and Madisons; Brittanys, Tiffanys, and Kimberlys; and the rest. Deep thought, long-term plans, and much energy goes into seeing to it that they get into the right colleges. ("Tufts somehow feels right for Ashley, Oberlin for Belmont.") What happens when they don't get into the right college, when they in effect fail to repay all the devout attention and care lavished upon them, is another, sadder story.

I began by talking about "fashions" in fatherhood, but I wonder if "fashions" is the right word. I wonder if "cultural imperatives" doesn't cover the case more precisely. Since raising my sons in the hodgepodge way I did, I have become a grandfather, with two grandchildren living in northern California and one, a granddaughter now in her twenties, living in Chicago. My second (and final) wife and I have had a fairly extensive hand in helping to bring up our Chicago granddaughter, and I have to admit that, even though there is much about it with which I disagree, we have done so largely under the arrangements of the new parenting regime.

When this charming child entered the game, I had long since been working at home, with a loose enough schedule to allow me to bring up my granddaughter in a manner that violated just about everything I have mocked both in person and now in print about the way children are currently brought up. I drove her to school and lessons and usually picked her up afterward. I helped arrange private schools for her. I spent at least thrice the time with her that I did with my two sons combined. I heartily approved all her achievements. Yes—I report this with head bowed—when she was six-years-old I took her to Disneyland; and, worse news, I rather enjoyed it.

Not the "debbil," as the comedian Flip Wilson used to say, but the culture made me become nothing less than a hovering, endlessly bothering, in-her-face grandfather. (Pause for an old Freudian joke: Why do grandparents and grandchildren get on so well? Answer: Because they have a common enemy.) The culture of his day condoned my father in his certainty that his business came before all else, allowing him to become an honorable if inattentive parent. The culture of my day allowed me to be a mildly muddled if ultimately responsible parent and still not entirely loathe myself. The culture of the current day dictated my bringing up my granddaughter, as I did with my wife's extensive help, as a nearly full-time job.

The culture of the current day calls for fathers to put in quite as much time with their children as mothers once did. In part this is owing to the fact that more and more women with children either need or want to work, and in part because, somehow, it only seems fair. Today if a father does not attend the games of his children, he is delinquent. If a father fails to take a strong hand in his children's education, he is deficient. If a father does not do all in his power to build up his children's self-esteem—"Good job, Ian"—he is damnable. If a father does not regularly hug and kiss his children and end all phone calls with "love ya," he is a monster. These are the dictates of the culture on—shall we call it?—"fathering" in our day, and it is not easy to go up against them; as an active grandparent, I, at least, did not find it easy.

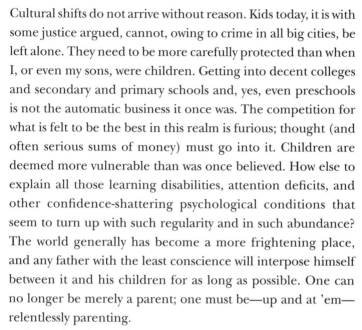

Cultural shifts do not arrive without reason. Kids today, it is with some justice argued, cannot, owing to crime in all big cities, be left alone. They need to be more carefully protected than when I, or even my sons, were children. Getting into decent colleges and secondary and primary schools and, yes, even preschools is not the automatic business it once was. The competition for what is felt to be the best in this realm is furious; thought (and often serious sums of money) must go into it. Children are deemed more vulnerable than was once believed. How else to explain all those learning disabilities, attention deficits, and other confidence-shattering psychological conditions that seem to turn up with such regularity and in such abundance? The world generally has become a more frightening place, and any father with the least conscience will interpose himself between it and his children for as long as possible. One can no longer be merely a parent; one must be—up and at 'em—relentlessly parenting.

As a university teacher I have encountered students brought up under this new, full-time attention regimen. On occasion, I have been amused by the unearned confidence of some of these kids. Part of me—the part Flip Wilson's debbil controls—used to yearn to let the air out of their self-esteem. How many wretchedly executed student papers have I read, at the bottom of which I wished to write, "F—too much love in the home."

Will all the attention showered on the current generation of children now make them smarter, more secure, finer, and nobler human beings? That remains, as the journalists used to say about the outcomes of Latin American revolutions, to be seen. Have the obligations of fathering made men's lives richer, or have they instead loaded men down with a feeling of hopeless inadequacy, for no man can hope to be the ideal father required in our day? How many men, one wonders, after a weekend of heavily programmed, rigidly regimented, fun fathering with the kids, can't wait to return to the simpler but genuine pleasures of work? Only when the cultural imperative of parenting changes yet again are we likely to know.

"He that hath wife and children," wrote Francis Bacon, "hath given hostages to fortune, for they are impediments to great enterprises, either of virtue or mischief." Yet many centuries earlier, when Croesus, the richest man of his day, asked the wise Solon who was the most contented man in the world, thinking Solon would answer him—Croesus—Solon surprised him by naming an otherwise obscure Athenian named Tellus. The reason this was so, Solon explained, is that "he lived at a time when his city was particularly well, he had handsome, upstanding sons, and he ended up a grandfather, with all his grandchildren making it to adulthood."

Fathering children puts a man under heavy obligation and leaves him vulnerable to endless worry, not only about the fate of his children but of his children's children. This being so, the most sensible thing, one might think, is not to have children. But one would think wrong. Not to have children cuts a man off from any true sense of futurity and means that he has engaged life less than fully. Fatherhood, for all its modern-day complications, is ultimately manhood.

About the Contributors

DAVID BURGE has successfully reproduced twice, resulting in a daughter (twenty-two) and a son (nineteen) far better than he deserves. He is also the proprietor of Iowahawk (iowahawk. typepad.com), considered by some to be one of the sites on the Internet. His writing has also appeared in the *Weekly Standard*, *Big Hollywood*, *Garage Magazine*, and *The Seven Deadly Virtues*. He lives in Austin, Texas, where his wife reminds you that fathering a child is the easy part.

CHRISTOPHER CALDWELL is a senior editor at the *Weekly Standard* and the author of *Reflections on the Revolution in Europe* (Doubleday/Penguin). His essays and reviews appear in many U.S. and European publications.

TUCKER CARLSON is the editor of the *Daily Caller* and the host of *Fox & Friends Weekend*. He and his wife have four children and two dogs. He likes to fly-fish.

MATTHEW CONTINETTI is editor-in-chief of FreeBeacon.com and a columnist for *Commentary* magazine.

JOSEPH EPSTEIN's most recent book is *Masters of the Games: Essays and Stories about Sports* (Rowman and Littlefield).

ANDREW FERGUSON is a senior editor at the *Weekly Standard* and the author most recently of *Crazy U: One Dad's Crash Course in Getting His Kid into College.*

JONAH GOLDBERG is a senior editor of *National Review* and a fellow at the American Enterprise Institute. A Fox News contributor, he is the author of two *New York Times* best sellers, *Liberal Fascism* and *The Tyranny of Clichés.* He is currently working on a new book that his dog, Zoë, has absolutely no interest in.

MICHAEL GRAHAM is a writer and radio talk-show host living in Atlanta, Georgia.

STEPHEN F. HAYES is a senior writer at the *Weekly Standard* and a Fox News contributor.

MATT LABASH is a senior writer at the *Weekly Standard.* His collection *Fly-Fishing with Darth Vader: And Other Adventures with Evangelical Wrestlers, Political Hitmen, and Jewish Cowboys* was published in 2010 by Simon & Schuster. He lives in Owings, Maryland.

JONATHAN V. LAST is a senior writer at the *Weekly Standard* and editor of *The Seven Deadly Virtues: 18 Conservative Writers on Why the Virtuous Life Is Funny as Hell.* In 2013 he published *What to Expect When No One's Expecting: America's Coming Demographic Disaster,* which is probably the funniest book ever written about fertility and demographics. He lives in Virginia with his wife and three children, and is, slowly, teaching the kids to surf.

JAMES LILEKS is a Metro columnist, blogger, and video producer for the *Star Tribune* in Minneapolis. He writes the "Athwart!" column in *National Review* and appears fortnightly on National Review Online. Full responsibility for the inordinately large pop-culture repository of lileks.com is his, and he writes "The Bleat" Monday to Friday at that very address. *The Casablanca Tango*, his latest, a newspaper-noir novel, can be found on amazon.com. He hates biographical paragraphs that end with some small, winsome detail, like this one.

ROB LONG is a writer and producer in Hollywood. He began his career writing and producing TV's long-running *Cheers*, and served as co-executive producer in its final season. During his time on the series, *Cheers* received two Emmy Awards and two Golden Globe Awards. Long has been nominated twice for an Emmy Award, and has received a Writers Guild of America Award. He continues to work in film and television in Los Angeles. His two books, *Conversations with My Agent* and *Set Up, Joke, Set Up, Joke*, were republished as a set in 2014 by Bloomsbury. Long is a contributing editor to *National Review* and a weekly columnist for the *National*, Abu Dhabi's English-language daily newspaper. His weekly radio commentary, "Martini Shot," is broadcast on the Los Angeles public radio station KCRW and is distributed nationally as a podcast. He is a co-founder of the fast-growing Ricochet.com, the place for smart and stimulating conversation—on the Web and mobile devices—from a center/right perspective.

LARRY MILLER is an actor, comedian, voice artist, podcaster, and columnist. He has appeared in over one hundred films and television shows, including *Seinfeld* and *10 Things I Hate about You*, as well as several characters in Christopher Guest's mockumentary films. His other credits include *Pretty Woman*, *The Nutty Professor*, *Nutty Professor II: The Klumps*, *Law & Order*, and *Boston Legal*. In addition, he's a contributing humorist to the *Huffington Post* and the *Weekly Standard*, as well as the author of the best-selling book *Spoiled Rotten America*. Miller hosts the podcast *The Larry Miller Show*, where he unleashes a barrage of humor about the absurdities of daily life.

P. J. O'ROURKE is the author, most recently, of *The Baby Boom: How It Got That Way . . . And It Wasn't My Fault . . . And I'll Never Do It Again*. He is a regular contributor to the *Weekly Standard* and the *Daily Beast* and an H. L. Mencken Fellow at the Cato Institute. But, first and foremost, he is the proud father of a daughter, Muffin, age seventeen; a daughter, Poppet, age fourteen; and a son, whatsisname, who's ten or eleven or something like that.

JOE QUEENAN writes the "Moving Targets" column for the *Wall Street Journal*. Author of nine books, he is a graduate of St. Joseph's College in Philadelphia. He has two children: a lawyer and a doctor of neuroscience.

TOBY YOUNG has worked as a feature writer, a film critic, a political columnist, and a judge on *Top Chef* over the course of his thirty-year career as a journalist. He is the author of *How to Lose Friends and Alienate People*, a memoir about his adventures at *Vanity Fair* magazine in New York, and co-produced the film of the same name. He is currently an associate editor of the *Spectator*, where he has written a weekly column since 1998.